SOUP

101 Productions Cookbooks

These titles can be ordered directly from the publisher:
The Cole Group, Inc., 4415 Sonoma Highway, Santa Rosa, CA 95409, (707) 538-0495

They are available at your local bookstores or wholesalers nationwide through:
Publishers Group West, 4065 Hollis, Emeryville, CA 94608, (800) 788-3123

And for gift and gourmet retailers, department stores and housewares merchants through:
Profiles Books, P.O. Box 5553, Kent, WA 98064, (800) 451-7647

In Canada please contact:
McClelland & Stewart, Inc., 380 Esna Park Drive, Markham, Ontario, CAN L3R 1H5
(800) 268-5748, or (800) 268-5707 (from Ontario and Quebec)

SOUP

Coralie Castle
Illustrations by
Roy Killeen

101

101 PRODUCTIONS

Publisher Brete Harrison
Associate Publisher James Connolly
Director of Production Steve Lux
Production Assistant Dotti Hydue
Front and Back Cover photography Michael Lamotte
Illustrations Roy Killeen

Distributed to the book trade by Publishers Group West

Printed and bound in the USA
Published by 101 Productions/The Cole Group
4415 Sonoma Highway, PO Box 4089
Santa Rosa, CA 95402-4089
(707) 538-0492 FAX (707) 538-0497

A   B   C   D   E   F   G   H
3   4   5   6   7   8   9   0
Library of Congress Catalog Card Number 92-30791

ISBN 1-56426-552-8

Contents

Spirit of
Soups Past

Some foods are for lovers,
some for philosophers,
some for tax collectors . . .
When one is near the grave,
I prepare for him some lentil soup,
and make the crowning meal
of his life glorious
          —Athenaeus 200 B.C.

Soup is considered to be the most ancient of foods, but its beginning is hard to trace. Archeologists never mention soup, probably because it didn't fossilize, carbonize, desiccate or leave traces in mummified stomachs.

Just as man was learning to write and record his own history, an ancient Egyptian cook let a bowl of gruel stand too long in the sun, thereby inventing beer. Soon after came mead from honey, wine from grapes, and distilled liquors. Ever since, intrigued writers have been so busy turning out volumes extolling or damning these social beverages, they've had little time or interest left for lowly soup.

Esau, in selling his birthright to Jacob for the pottage of red lentils, was considered a fool. Elisha performed a miracle when he cast meal into a pottage of poisonous boiled wild gourds "and then there was no harm in it." The Israelites made a purée of manna, the secretion of small insects on twigs of the tamarisk, but there is little other biblical reference to soup except when Isaiah wrote, "and broth of abominable things is in their vessels."

References to soups show up all over the world. As far back as 200 B.C., Vedic literature in India mentioned parched barley ground up with juices. Mayan Indians used maize for various liquid foods, most at least mildly alcoholic. Early North American Indians made a broth of hickory-nut milk. Yosemite Indians shredded fungi for mushroom soup and also cooked horse-chestnut gruel. Eskimos still relish soup laced with seal or caribou blood.

ANCIENT GREECE AND ROME

The Greeks and Romans produced a few historians interested in all kinds of food, including soup. By 600 B.C. in Greece, soups of beans, peas or lentils relieved the monotony of "bread and a relish," and hot pea soup could be bought in the streets. Kykeon (barley gruel, water and aromatic herbs like pennyroyal, mint or thyme) served as a ritual beverage at the mysteries of Eleusis. Black broth, made of pork, blood, vinegar, salt and heavy seasoning was a main dish.

Apicius, a first-century Roman, wrote the earliest cookbook still in existence. His barley soup was made by boiling crushed barley with lentils, peas and chickpeas. He mentions a purée of lettuce and onions. There was also a liquid sweet fruit dish of apricots cooked in honey, passum (dried grapes and must), wine and vinegar flavored with pepper, mint and a little liquamen (strained liquid from salted-down fish entrails, available commercially in trademarked pots as early as 400 B.C.). Apicius is said to have killed himself when his fortune ran out and he could no longer afford expensive, rare foods.

It was Athenaeus in 200 A.D. who wrote the most about food, seasonings and soup. His *Deipnosophists* (*deipno,* meaning dining and *sophist,* sage) recounts endless dinner conversations that range over many subjects. Here are a few samples:

" 'No Lentils bring to me. They do taint the breath—no expensive dishes, but any of those vulgar lentils or what is called lentil soup.' And when everyone laughed, especially at the idea of lentil soup, he said, 'You are very ignorant men, you feasters, never having read any books of the Silli of Timon the Pyrrhonian. For he speaks of lentil soup as follows':

> *"The Teian barley-cakes do please me not,*
> *Nor e'en the Lydian sauces: but the Greeks,*
> *And their dry lentil soup, delight me more*
> *Than all that painful luxury of excess."*

THE MIDDLE AGES TO MODERN SOUPS

In early times soup was called pottage (from pot and the latin *potare,* to drink). But during the Middle Ages the word "soup" (thought to be onomatopoeic of the sound of slurping hot liquid from a spoon) established itself in every European language, largely supplanting "pottage" except for *potage* in France. Some variations are: *soop, sopa, sope, soepe, suppa, soppe, soep, suppe, soppa, sopero, soupe, chupe, zuppa, zup.* To "sup" was to eat the evening meal at which soup was traditionally served, and the meal itself became "supper."

In 1475, a Venetian by the name of Platina published *De Honesta Voluptate,* a cookbook and guide to living with "honest indulgence and good health." With complete candor, he commented on the merits of various foods. For example, according to him, lentils generate black bile and cause leprosy, while turnips "soothe the throat and arouse the passion."

His soup recipes range from potages of livers, lungs and intestines to Verzusum, a sweet soup that "cools the liver and checks the bile." It required thirty egg yolks to make his saffron broth; white broth contained a pound of ground almonds, twenty egg whites and softened white bread. Soups were always to be kept far enough away from the coals so as not to absorb the smoke. Many of them called for verjuice (acid liquor from sour fruit juice) or must (unfermented wine). Even though he said hemp potage was difficult to digest and caused squeamishness, its elaborate recipe was included, as well as one for an eel torta, which was to be served to one's enemies because it was so bad.

In 1669, *The CLOSET of the Eminent Learned Sir Kenelme Digbie Kt.* was published in London, and contained the following soup recipes:

"Barley Potage—Take half a pound of French-barley, and wash it in three or four hot waters; then tye it up in a course linnen-cloth and strike it five or six blows against the table; for this will make it very tender . . . and let it mittoner a while upon the Chafing-dish, then serve it in. . . .

"Portugal Broth, as it was made for the Queen— Make a very good broth with some lean of Veal, Beef and Mutton, and with a brawny Hen or Young Cock . . . and when the broth is very good, you may drink it so, or, pour a little of it upon tosted sliced bread, and stew it, till the bread have drunk up all that broth, then add a little more, and stew; so adding by little and little, that the bread may imbibe it and swell: whereas if you drown it at once, the bread will not swell, and grow like gelly.

"Potage de santé of Mounsieur de S.—Put a knuckle of Veal and a Hen into an earthen Pipkkin with a Gallon of water (about nine of the Clock forenoon) and boil it gently. When no more scum riseth (which will be in about a quarter of an hour,) take out the Hen (which else would be too much boiled,) and continue boiling gently till about half an hour past ten. Then put in the Hen again, and a handful of white Endive. Near half hour after eleven, put in two good handfuls of tender Sorrel, Borage, Bugloss, Lettuce, Purslane a handful a piece, a little Cerfevil, and a little Beet-leaves. When he is in pretty good health, that he may venture upon more savoury hotter things, he puts in a large Onion stuck round with Cloves, and sometimes a little bundle of Thyme and other hot savoury herbs; which let boil a good half hour or better, and take them out, and throw them away. . . ."

During the eighteenth century, references to soup occasionally appeared in English literature. In 1724, a manual on swift service advised, "Let the Cook daub the Back of his new Livery; or when he is going up with a Dish of Soup, let her follow him softly with a Ladle-full." Also, in the mid 1700s, the British navy developed its famous "portable soup, a grey, dehydrated powder which will keep in canisters indefinitely."

By the nineteenth century, the word "soup" had become the source of some strange expressions. The term "soup-shop," according to the *London Journal,* referred to those establishments where burglars and thieves disposed of any silver or gold plate which fell into their hands. In such places, the melting pots were always kept ready. In Ireland, Protestant clergymen who sought converts by dispensing soup as charity were called "soupers." In 1890, the *Catholic News* commented, "Our readers are no doubt aware of the usual falsehoods employed by soupers for this purpose."

Meanwhile, 1890 Chicagoans were presumably poring over a newly published *Compendium of Cookery together with the Book of Knowledge, or 1000 ways of getting rich.* Along with the Bible it apparently handled all of life's problems. It offers a "tonic for reformed drunkards to restore the vigor of the stomach." On the other hand it prescribes: "Fever and Ague—Four ounces galangal-root in a quart of gin, steeped in a warm place; take often."

More intriguing is its advice on how "To Restore From Stroke of Lightning—Shower with cold water for two hours; if the patient does not show signs of life, put salt in the water, and continue to shower an hour

longer." What then? Its soups section sounds a little more practical:

"*Stock Soup*—. . . basis of many of the soups. . . . Time: Five and one-half hours. Average cost, twenty-five cents per quart. . . .

"*White Stock Soup*—. . . Strain off the liquor; rub the vegetables through the colander . . . and, as is your Saturday custom, put into a wide-mouth jar or a large bowl. . . .

"Potatoes, if boiled in the soup, are thought by some to render it unwholesome, from the opinion that the water in which potatoes have been cooked is almost a poison. . . .

"*Mutton Soup*—Three pounds perfectly lean mutton. The scrag makes good soup and costs little. Two or three pounds of bones well pounded. . . . Send around grated cheese with this soup. . . .

"*Chicken Cream Soup*—Boil an old fowl, with an onion, in four quarts of cold water, until there remain but two quarts. . . .

"*Potato Soup*—Get as many beef or ham bones as you can, and smash them into fragments. . . .

"*Game Soup*—Two grouse or partridges, or if you have neither, use a pair of rabbits. . . ."

Simultaneously in San Francisco was published: *Scammell's Universal Treasure-House of Useful Knowledge,* "an Encyclopedia of Valuable Receipts in the Principal Arts of Life, including complete treatises on Practical chemistry; the prevention and cure of disease; household and culinary art; agriculture and stock-raising; the mechanical arts; mercantile life and laws; arts of refinement; recreations, etc." The soups include:

"*Calf's Head*—Parboil a calf's head; take off the skin and cut it into pieces of about 1-1/2" square; mince the fleshy part into smaller pieces; take out the back part of the eyes, and cut the remainder into rings; skin the tongue; cut it into slices; turn the whole into 3 qts of good stock. . . .

"*Celery*—9 heads of celery; 1 teaspoonful of salt, nutmeg to taste; 1 lump of sugar; 1/2 pt of strong stock; 1 pt. of cream; 2 qts. of boiling water; cut the celery into small pieces; throw it into the water. . . .

"*Lentil*—Take 3/4 lb. of lentils; pick, wash and set on the fire with cold water, just enough to cover; do not cook in an earthen pot, as they will not get soft. . . .

"*Consommé*—6 lbs of lean beef; an old fowl, with the giblets, and any pieces of bone that you may have. . . .

"*Curry*—Cut the meat from an ox cheek; soak it well. . . .

"*French*—Clean nicely a sheep's head . . . strain all off; cut the head into pieces and serve in the soup. . . .

"*Herb*—Slice 3 large but young cucumbers; a handful of spring onions and six lettuces. . . .

"*Mock Turtle*—Take 1/2 a calf's head . . . procure a tin of mock turtle soup, boil this up with stock. . . . The mixture of the stock made from fresh vegetables, with the preserved soup, will correct the slight taste of tin, which is the only objection which can be urged against it; and when a small quantity only of soup is required it will save time, trouble and expense to make it in this way, rather than to prepare it at home."

For years cookbook writers apparently felt responsibility for far more than food, and readers valued such books highly.

Published in 1905, *The White House Cook Book,* "a comprehensive cyclopedia of information for the home containing cooking, toilet and household recipes, menus, dinner-giving, table etiquette, care of the sick, health suggestions, facts worth knowing, etc.," was dedicated "To the wives of Our Presidents, those noble women who have graced the White House." One copy was inscribed by its owner, "This book belongs to Mrs. Nellie P. Doane, she wants it and needs it and is a scratching, biting, kicking hairpuller. So beware."

Among the soup recipes are the following:

"Plain Economical Soup—Take a cold roast-beef bone etc. . . . Serve this soup with sippits of toast. Sippits are bits of dry toast cut into a triangular form. A seasonable dish about the holidays. . . .

"Squirrel Soup—Wash and quarter three or four good sized squirrels; put them on, with a small tablespoonful of salt, directly after breakfast in a gallon of cold water. Cover the pot close. . . .

"Green Turtle Soup—After removing the entrails, cut up the coarser parts of the turtle meat and bones. Add four quarts of water. . . . At the end of four hours strain the soup, and add the inner parts of the turtle and the green fat. . . . If there are eggs in the turtle, boil them in a separate vessel for four hours, and throw into the soup before taking up. . . . Some cooks put in the green fat, cut into lumps an inch long. This makes a handsomer soup. Green turtle can now be purchased preserved in air-tight cans."

The Corona Club Cookbook, published in San Francisco in 1910, contains the following:

"Wine Soup—One quart boiling water, 1/2 teacupful of sago, the peeling of 1/2 a lemon; boil until sago is done, then add 1 teacupful of claret wine and sugar to taste. . . .

"Barley Water—Teacup of pearl barley; add 2 quarts of water; boil in a double porcelain boiler 2-1/2 hours. Add 1 cup table raisins an hour before you remove it from the stove. It will look milky and a little thick. Squeeze the juice of 33 lemons in a pitcher, sweeten and salt it a little; strain the hot barley water over the above; pick out the raisins; put them in with the rest. Throw the barley away. To an invalid, it looks very inviting in a glass pitcher. Very acceptable to a fever patient. . . .

"Scraped Beef in Broth—Buy 1/4 of a pound of round steak; be careful none of the dried edges of the meat are included in your purchase, as this sometimes poisons babies. Sear on hot griddle to retain the juice. Split in two and scrape with a dull knife so that only the pulp and none of the fibre is retained. Put in broth with rice."

According to Escoffier, soups were considered commonplace until this century. Only recently have they been perfected and firmly established as part of a fashionable meal. Our ancestors would be amazed and delighted, I think, if they were to taste all of the varied soups that follow.

Stocks and Light Soups

"One wit, like a knuckle of ham in the soup, gives zest to the dish, but more than one serves only to spoil the pottage."

—Tobias Smollett

Simmer selected raw, pre-cooked or leftover morsels in water with butter or wine. Skim, strain out the leached solids, and season if desired. Cool, then refrigerate. Remove the solidified fat and you have the liquor so vital to every soup chef—stock.

Sounds simple—until you consider the complexity of possible ingredients and flavors. While proportions are inexact, merely tossing anything and everything into a pot is not the answer. The ingredients must be good ones and they must be treated with care.

Broth is simply stock that has been reduced by longer cooking, thus concentrating the flavor. A consommé is more concentrated still, plus it is enriched by the addition of ingredients beyond those used in simple stocks and it must be clarified.

If your butcher bones your roasts or chicken breasts, be sure to ask him to wrap the bones and scraps for your stock pot.

BASICS OF MAKING STOCKS

LEFTOVERS Bones, scraps, carcasses, unserved portions, gravies, vegetable cooking water, vegetable tops, leaves and scrapings all are valuable in making stock as long as they're clean and kept refrigerated until added to the pot. Recycling in the kitchen is more than just an economy, it's a system of flavor saving, of cooking with your own array of delicious concentrates that are continually being modified, added to, and blended. Stocks are the flavor key not only to soups, but to many other dishes as well. For example, boiling fresh vegetables in stock instead of plain water.

COOKING Cut up bones if possible. Start with cold water, cover, bring slowly to a rapid boil. Skim off any scum that rises to the surface. Turn down the heat and simmer, covered, 2 hours for leftover bones, 4 hours for fresh, adding vegetables and seasoning at the halfway point. Strain through coarse sieve into another kettle, then through a finer one into jars. Cool completely, put lids on jars, label and refrigerate.

STORING Fat acts as a sealer and solidifies under refrigeration, making it easy to remove. If stock is not used within one week, it's best to return it to the pot for a two-minute boil, after which it can be refrigerated again. To freeze, pour stock into containers, leaving an inch and a half head space, and top with an airtight lid. Freeze no longer than four months. Thaw and remove fat. Because freezing causes ingredients to separate, bring the stock to a boil before using.

DEFATTING If fresh stock is to be used immediately, skim off as much surface fat as possible, then float an ice cube in the stock to congeal the rest. A piece of chilled lettuce will collect fat on its surface.

Worcestershire and soy sauce and Maggi's seasoning add color and a salty flavor.

CLARIFYING To each quart of stock add 1 egg white beaten slightly with 2 teaspoons cold water and 1 crumbled egg shell. Stir and heat to boiling. Boil 2 minutes, remove from heat and let stand without stirring 20 minutes. Pour through strainer lined with double cheesecloth.

CONCENTRATING For richer, more flavorful stock or broth, boil down strained stock to reduce water content.

• To make frozen concentrate, boil down until very strong, but still pourable. Freeze in ice cube trays or small containers.

• To make seasoning base, boil down until very thick and concentrated. Refrigerate in covered jar for up to five days. Use to add extra flavor.

A gelatinous stock (made by filling your stock pot with an extra measure of fresh bones) is excellent for nutrition but disastrous for making cold soups.

• To make mushroom concentrate, soften 1 ounce dried mushrooms in warm water to cover. Drain, reserving water, and mince. Sauté 3 ounces fresh mushroom stems, minced, in 2 teaspoons butter until golden, sprinkling with 1/8 teaspoon *each* salt and ground oregano. Add water to reserved soaking water to make 1-1/2 cups and add to pan with minced softened mushrooms and 2 teaspoons soy sauce. Bring to boil and cook until liquid is reduced to 1/2 cup. Strain, pressing liquid out of mushrooms. Cover and store in refrigerator.

• To make creamy mushroom concentrate, combine mushroom concentrate with 2 tablespoons rice flour. Heat and add 1/4 cup heavy cream. Cool, cover and refrigerate.

Stocks from Fresh Fresh Bones

2 pounds veal knuckle bone with meat, cut up
2 pounds veal shin bones, cut up
1 pair pig's feet
4 quarts water
2 carrots, chopped
2 onions, unpeeled and quartered
2 leeks, chopped (white and some green)
2 ribs celery and leaves, chopped
2 turnips, chopped (optional)
2 garlic cloves (optional)
6 sprigs parsley
1 sprig thyme
1 bay leaf
2 teaspoons salt
6 black peppercorns, lightly crushed
1/2 teaspoon ground turmeric

WHITE STOCK

Cover bones and pig's feet with 2 quarts of the water, bring to rapid boil, drain and rinse bones. Return to clean soup kettle and add remaining water. Cover, bring slowly to rapid boil and skim off any surface scum. Lower heat, cover and simmer 2 hours.

Add remaining ingredients and simmer 2 more hours. Strain, jar, cool, cover and refrigerate.

BROWN VEAL STOCK

Brown bones and feet in 3 tablespoons oil and/or butter or rendered chicken fat in soup kettle or oven. Simmer 2 hours with water. Brown vegetables (peel onion), add and continue cooking 2 more hours.

BEEF STOCK

4 pounds beef bones with meat, cut up
1 to 2 pounds marrow bones, sawed into 3-inch pieces
1 pair pig's feet
5 quarts water
3 carrots, chopped
2 ribs celery and leaves, chopped
2 turnips, chopped
2 whole onions, each stuck with 2 whole cloves
2 ripe tomatoes, chopped (optional)
1/4 cup diced bell pepper (optional)
6 sprigs parsley
1 sprig thyme
1 sprig oregano or marjoram
1 bay leaf
2 large garlic cloves (optional)
6 black peppercorns, lightly crushed
1 tablespoon salt

Cover bones and pig's feet with 2 quarts of the water, bring to rapid boil, drain and rinse bones and feet. Return to clean soup kettle, add remaining water, cover, bring slowly to rapid boil and skim off any surface scum. Lower heat, cover and simmer for 2 hours.

Add rest of ingredients and continue cooking 2 more hours. Strain, jar, cool, cover and refrigerate.

DARK BEEF STOCK

Brown bones in butter and/or oil or rendered beef fat in soup kettle or hot oven. Simmer 2 hours with water. Brown vegetables (peel onion), add and continue cooking 2 hours.

When a recipe calls for a whole onion, do not peel.

CHICKEN STOCK

6 pounds chicken backs, necks and wing tips, cut up
3 quarts cold water
2 onions, unpeeled and quartered
2 carrots, chopped
1 turnip, chopped
2 ribs celery and leaves, chopped
2 leeks, (white and some green)
2 garlic cloves
1 bay leaf
6 sprigs parsley
1 sprig thyme
1 sprig savory
1 tablespoon salt
1 teaspoon ground turmeric
1/2 teaspoon poultry seasoning

WHITE STOCK

Put bones and water in soup kettle, cover, bring slowly to rapid boil and skim off any surface scum. Lower heat, cover and simmer 2 hours.

Add remaining ingredients and simmer 2 more hours. Strain, jar, cool, cover and refrigerate.

BROWN CHICKEN STOCK

Brown bones in 3 tablespoons butter and/or rendered chicken fat in kettle or hot oven. Simmer 2 hours with water. Brown vegetables (peel onion), add and continue cooking 2 more hours.

OXTAIL STOCK

2-1/2 pounds oxtails, cut up
1/4 pound ham, diced
1-1/2 cups chopped celery and some leaves
1 cup chopped carrot
3/4 cup chopped onion
1/2 cup chopped turnip
1/4 cup chopped leek (white and some green)
3 tablespoons rendered beef fat and/or butter
8 cups water
2 sprigs savory
2 sprigs thyme
4 sprigs parsley
2 tablespoons tomato paste
1 cup port wine
1 teaspoon salt
1/2 teaspoon black pepper

Sauté oxtails, ham and vegetables in beef fat over high heat, stirring constantly, until browned. Add water, herbs, tomato paste, wine, salt and pepper. Cover, bring to gentle boil and cook 2-1/2 to 3 hours, or until oxtails are tender. During cooking, skim off any scum that rises to surface. Remove oxtails, strain, cool, jar, cover and refrigerate. Reserve meat from oxtails for use in soups, or serve oxtails as a meat course.

PORK STOCK

Follow directions for Chicken Stock (preceding), substituting pork bones for chicken bones and sage for turmeric; add 1 oregano sprig.

LAMB STOCK

Follow directions for Beef Stock (page 15), substituting lamb blocks or other bones for the beef and adding 1 sprig rosemary.

Stocks from Leftover Bones

POULTRY STOCK

1 turkey carcass, or 2 chicken, duck or geese carcasses, plus any leftover scraps and giblets
2 onions, unpeeled and quartered
2 carrots, chopped
2 leeks, chopped (white and some green)
2 turnips, chopped
1 garlic clove
6 sprigs parsley
1 sprig thyme
1 bay leaf
6 black peppercorns, lightly crushed
1/2 tablespoon salt
1/2 teaspoon *each* poultry seasoning and ground turmeric
3 quarts water

Put all ingredients in soup kettle, cover, bring slowly to rapid boil and skim off any surface scum. Lower heat, cover and simmer 2 hours. Strain, jar, cool, cover and refrigerate.

17

GAME STOCK

4 pounds venison bones and scraps, or pheasant or partridge carcasses, or rabbit bones, plus scraps and giblets (add veal knuckle bone if needed to make 4 pounds)
2 onions, unpeeled and quartered
2 carrots, chopped
2 ribs celery and leaves, chopped
1/4 pound salt pork, diced and blanched
2 garlic cloves
1 teaspoon salt
6 sprigs parsley
1 sprig thyme
1 bay leaf
2 whole cloves
1 teaspoon minced fresh basil
4 black peppercorns, lightly crushed
1/2 teaspoon juniper berries, lightly crushed
3 quarts cold water

Put all ingredients in soup kettle. Cover, bring slowly to rapid boil and skim off any surface scum. Lower heat, cover and simmer 2 hours. Strain and boil to reduce to 2 quarts or less, as desired.

Jar, cool, cover and refrigerate. Remove fat and clarify before using.

STOCK FROM RIB ROAST OF BEEF

2 onions, unpeeled and quartered
2 carrots, chopped
2 ribs celery and leaves, chopped
2 leeks, chopped (white and some green)
2 garlic cloves (optional)
3 tablespoons oil and/or rendered beef fat
6 or 7 cracked ribs of leftover rib roast of beef and any scraps
6 black peppercorns, lightly crushed
8 sprigs parsley
1 sprig thyme
1 sprig marjoram
1 bay leaf
1/2 tablespoon salt
1 tablespoon mushroom concentrate (page 14)
2 quarts cold water

Brown onions, carrots, celery, leeks and garlic in oil. Add to soup kettle with rest of ingredients, cover, bring slowly to rapid boil and skim off any surface scum. Lower heat, cover and simmer 2 hours. Strain, jar, cool, cover and refrigerate.

LAMB STOCK

Follow directions for Stock from Rib Roast of Beef (preceding), using leftover leg of lamb bones and scraps for the beef bones; add 1 sprig rosemary and 1 sprig oregano.

PORK STOCK

Follow directions for Stock from Rib Roast of Beef (preceding), using leftover pork bones for the beef bones; add 2 teaspoons minced fresh sage and 1 sprig oregano.

FISH STOCK

2 cups *each* white wine and water
2 pounds fish heads, bones, shells from non-oily fish
1 onion, chopped
3 sprigs parsley
1 bay leaf
1 sprig thyme
2 tablespoons fresh lemon juice
1 teaspoon minced fresh tarragon
1 teaspoon freshly grated lemon peel
6 black peppercorns, lightly crushed
2 whole cloves
1/2 cup mushroom stems, or 1 tablespoon mushroom concentrate (page 14)
1 teaspoon salt
1 tablespoon butter or safflower oil

Combine ingredients in kettle, cover, bring slowly to rapid boil and skim off any surface scum. Lower heat, cover and simmer 1 hour. Strain, jar, cool, cover and refrigerate no more than 4 days.

PETITE MARMITE

Follow general rules for making stock, using 1-1/2 pounds rump beef, cubed, 1 meaty veal knuckle, cut up, 2 beef bones, cut up, 4 chicken backs, 2-1/2 quarts water, 1 tablespoon salt, 3 black peppercorns, lightly crushed, 4 sprigs parsley and 1 sprig thyme. Cook 1 hour, add 2 carrots, chopped, 1 turnip, chopped, 1 leek, chopped (white and some green), 1 whole onion, stuck with 2 whole cloves, and 1 cup chopped celery and leaves. Cook 2 hours, strain, chill, defat and clarify.

BOUILLON

Follow recipe for Dark Beef Stock (page 15), adding 1 pound beef, cut up, and 1 meaty veal knuckle. Simmer 5 hours, strain, chill, defat and clarify. Add dry sherry and Worcestershire sauce to taste.

BEEF CONSOMME

Follow recipe for Dark Beef Stock (page 15), adding 1 large meaty veal knuckle and 4 chicken backs. Strain, reduce to concentrate flavor, chill, defat and clarify.

CHICKEN CONSOMME

Follow recipe for Brown Chicken Stock (page 16), adding 1 additional pound chicken backs and wings. Strain, reduce to concentrate flavor, chill, defat and clarify.

No time to chill your stock before defatting it? Simply let fat rise to top (about 5 minutes), scoop out as much as possible with a spoon and then float an ice cube or cold lettuce leaf on top. The remaining fat will attach itself to the cube or leaf. Remove and discard.

JELLIED BOUILLON

Soften 2 to 3 tablespoons unflavored gelatin in 1/2 cup cold water. Bring 4 cups Bouillon (preceding) to boil, add gelatin and stir to dissolve. Season with 1 teaspoon Worcestershire sauce and 2 tablespoons fresh lemon juice or dry white wine. Cool and chill until set. Break up with fork and serve with garnish of choice.

JELLIED MADRILENE

Combine 6 cups Brown Chicken Stock (page 16) or Veal Stock (page 15) with 2 cups tomato purée. Simmer 30 minutes and add 3 tablespoons unflavored gelatin softened in 1/4 cup *each* cold water and beet juice. Heat, stirring, to dissolve gelatin. Cool and chill until set. Break up with fork and serve with garnish of choice.

Vegetable Stocks

Vegetable stocks may be used interchangeably with meat-based stocks. They add a subtle, delicate flavor to any soup, and are an ideal way to use leftover vegetables in your refrigerator.

Store up to three days in the refrigerator and up to one month in the freezer.

VEGETABLE STOCK

1 large onion, unpeeled and quartered
2 leeks, chopped (white and some green)
2 ribs celery and leaves, chopped
2 carrots, chopped
4 tablespoons safflower oil or butter
2 potatoes, scrubbed and sliced
4 large garlic cloves, crushed
2 bay leaves
8 black peppercorns, lightly crushed
2 sprigs oregano
6 sprigs parsley
1 sprig thyme
1 sprig tarragon (optional)
4 whole cloves
6 cups water
3 ripe tomatoes, chopped (optional)
Salt to taste

Brown vegetables in oil in soup kettle. Add remaining ingredients, cover, bring to boil, lower heat and simmer 2 hours. Strain and adjust seasonings. Reduce to concentrate flavor. Jar, cool, cover and refrigerate.

VEGETABLE STOCK FROM LEFTOVERS

Use twice as much liquid, either plain water or water leftover from steaming vegetables or boiling potatoes, as cooked or raw vegetables, such as tomatoes, lettuce, parsnips, leeks, rutabagas, turnips, pods from shelled peas, green beans, carrots, onions, asparagus ends and green onion tops. Season with herbs and spices as desired. Follow directions for Vegetable Stock, preceding.

VEGETABLE CONSOMME

2 cups chopped onion
1 cup minced leeks (white and some green)
1/2 cup chopped celery root
1/2 cup chopped turnip and/or rutabaga
1 cup *each* chopped carrot and shredded cabbage
3 tablespoons butter
7 cups water
1 teaspoon salt
3 black peppercorns, lightly crushed
2 sprigs thyme
6 sprigs parsley
2 tablespoons minced fresh basil
Minced fresh herbs

Sauté vegetables in butter 10 minutes. Add water and seasonings, cover, bring to boil, lower heat and simmer 2 hours.

Strain, adjust seasonings to taste and serve hot or cold garnished with fresh herbs.

Vegetable peelings and mushroom and parsley stems have the most concentrated flavor and nutrients.

POTATO-GARLIC STOCK

20 to 24 garlic cloves, lightly crushed
1 onion, unpeeled and quartered
1 carrot, chopped
1 rib celery and leaves, chopped
1 turnip, chopped
4 potatoes, scrubbed and sliced
2 tablespoons safflower or olive oil
Extra potato peelings (optional)
6 cups water
1 bay leaf
3 sprigs parsley
1 sprig thyme or oregano
1 sprig sage or summer savory
6 white peppercorns, lightly crushed
Salt to taste

Lightly brown garlic, onion, carrot, celery and potatoes in oil in soup kettle. Add remaining ingredients, cover, bring to boil, lower heat and simmer 2 hours. Strain and adjust seasonings. Jar, cool, cover and refrigerate.

Lightly smash garlic clove with flat side of large knife blade. Peel comes off easily and garlic flavor is released.

Light Soups from Clear Stocks

The following recipes are refined uses of stocks and broths, the latter more flavorful, concentrated clear soups. You may or may not clarify the stocks and broths, as you wish.

CELERY BROTH

Serves 6
1-1/2 cups chopped celery and some leaves
1/2 cup chopped white of leeks
2 large ripe tomatoes, diced
3 tablespoons butter
6 cups chicken stock
Minced fresh celery leaves

Cook vegetables in butter, covered, 20 minutes. Add stock and cook 30 minutes.

Strain, adjust seasonings and garnish with celery leaves.

DOUBLE MUSHROOM CONSOMME

Serves 6
2 large dried mushrooms, softened in water to cover with a pinch of sugar
6 cups chicken, beef and/or veal broth
3 green onions and tops, slivered
1/2 pound minced fresh mushrooms
Fresh lemon juice
Dry white wine
Salt
White pepper
Thinly sliced fresh mushrooms, rubbed with fresh lemon juice

Dice softened dried mushrooms and combine with broth, green onions and fresh mushrooms. Cover, bring to boil, lower heat and simmer 45 minutes. Strain, pushing as much pulp through sieve as possible.

Season with lemon juice, wine, salt and pepper and garnish with sliced mushrooms.

STRACCIATELLA

Serves 6
6 cups beef broth or Beef Consommé (page 20)
6 eggs, beaten
1-1/3 cups freshly grated Parmesan or Romano cheese
1/2 teaspoon salt
1/4 teaspoon black pepper
1 tablespoon minced fresh Italian parsley
Minced fresh chives

Bring broth to boil and adjust seasonings to taste.

Beat together eggs, cheese, salt, pepper and parsley. Gradually pour into boiling soup, stirring with a fork to make ribbons of egg. Cook a few minutes to set eggs. Serve garnished with minced chives.

VARIATION Add cooked tripolini and garnish with diced tomato.

Italian parsley is not as attractive as the curly variety, but it has more flavor and is just as easy to grow.

CHICKEN BROTH WITH MUSHROOMS

Serves 6
6 cups chicken broth
1 cup diced cooked chicken
1/2 cup sliced mushrooms,
    sautéed in 1 tablespoon
    butter
1/4 pound cooked thin
    noodles or rice
Fresh lemon juice to taste
Minced fresh chervil or
    watercress

Bring broth to boil and adjust seasonings to taste. Add chicken, mushrooms, and noodles. Reheat and season with lemon juice. Garnish with chervil.

CHICKEN BROTH WITH GIBLETS

Serves 6
6 cups chicken broth
1 tablespoon mushroom
    concentrate (page 14)
1/2 cup *each* chopped onion,
    carrot and celery and leaves
1/4 cup diced core of
    cauliflower
2 leaves cabbage, shredded
1 bay leaf
6 sprigs parsley
Giblets from 2 or 3 chickens
Minced fresh parsley

Simmer broth, mushroom concentrate, vegetables, bay leaf and parsley, covered, 1 hour. Strain, return to soup kettle and bring to boil. Slice hearts and gizzards and add to boiling broth; cook 15 minutes.

Halve the livers, add to broth and cook 5 minutes. Sprinkle with parsley.

TURKEY BROTH WITH AVOCADO

Serves 6
6 cups turkey broth
2 avocados, diced, sliced or
    cut into rings
Fresh lemon juice
Minced fresh parsley

Heat broth to boiling and adjust seasonings to taste. Sprinkle avocados with lemon juice and just before serving add to hot broth. Garnish with minced parsley.

VARIATION You may lace with dry sherry.

SORREL BROTH

Serves 6
2 cups firmly packed minced
    fresh sorrel
6 cups chicken broth
3 eggs, beaten
1/4 cup dry sherry
Minced fresh parsley
Herb croutons

Simmer sorrel and broth 10
minutes.

Whisk 1/2 cup hot broth
into beaten eggs and return
to rest of soup. Reheat without boiling.

Adjust seasonings to taste,
add sherry, sprinkle with parsley and serve with herb
croutons.

VARIATION Add finely shredded
lettuce and minced fresh chervil to the broth and sorrel.

CONSOMME BRUNOISE

Serves 6
1/4 cup *each* finely shredded
    carrots, leeks and turnips
1/4 cup *each* thinly sliced
    celery and cauliflower
2 tablespoons butter
6 cups Beef or Chicken
    Consommé (page 20)
1/4 cup minced fresh parsley
Lemon peel slivers

Sauté vegetables in butter
until just tender-crisp. Heat
consommé and add vegetables.
Stir in parsley and garnish
with lemon peel.

*When chopping green-leaf
vegetables, such as sorrel and
Swiss chard, remove tough
stems and center veins first.*

POACHED EGG CONSOMME OR BROTH

Serves 6
6 cups Beef or Chicken
    Consommé (page 20) or
    broth
6 whole eggs
Finely minced fresh chives,
    parsley or chervil
Toast or croutons

Bring consommé to boil and
adjust seasonings. Break an
egg into 6 heated bowls and
pour hot soup over to poach
lightly. Garnish with chives,
and serve with toast.

NOTE Eggs can be poached
first if firmer eggs are desired

CONSOMME PRINCESSE

Serves 6

6 cups Chicken or Beef
  Consommé (page 20)
1/2 cup shelled green peas or
  asparagus tips
1/2 cup shredded cooked
  chicken
1/4 cup freshly grated Parmesan cheese
Minced fresh chervil

Bring consommé to boil; adjust
seasonings to taste. Add peas
and cook until just tender-
crisp. Add chicken and heat
through. Sprinkle with cheese
and chervil.

CONSOMME PRINTANIER

Serves 6

6 cups Beef or Chicken
  Consommé (page 20)
3 tablespoons *each* julienned
  turnips and carrots,
  blanched and drained
1/2 cup *each* cooked green
  peas and julienned French-
  cut green beans
Minced fresh chervil
Lemon slices

Bring consommé to boil, add
turnips and carrots and cook
until almost done. Add peas
and beans and reheat. Vegetables should be tender-crisp.
  Sprinkle with chervil and
serve with lemon slices.

VARIATIONS Substitute cooked
asparagus tips and/or small
kidney beans for peas and
green beans.

CELERY ROOT CONSOMME

Serves 6
1 large celery root, peeled
  and sliced 1/8 inch thick
6 cups Beef or Chicken
  Consommé (page 20)
Fresh lemon juice
Minced fresh parsley

Reserve 3 slices of celery root, cut them into julienne and soak them in cold water and lemon juice.

Simmer consommé and remaining celery root slices 1 hour, strain and return to soup kettle. Drain julienned celery root, add to kettle and cook until just tender-crisp.

Sprinkle with parsley.

To cut into julienne means to cut into matchstick-size pieces.

FUZZY MELON SOUP

A light, before-dinner broth with a delicate flavor that cannot be duplicated.

Serves 6
1 fuzzy melon (about 1/2
  pound)
6 cups Basic Chinese Chicken
  or Pork Broth (page 105)
1 tablespoon dried shrimp*
1 egg, beaten
*See glossary

Scrape fuzz off melon and cut melon into bite-size slices. Simmer stock and shrimp 20 minutes. Bring stock to boil, add melon, and cook 5 minutes after stock returns to boil.

Drizzle egg into soup and cook and stir 2 minutes. The egg should form long, slender strands.

QUICK WATERCRESS SOUP

Serves 4 to 6
4 cups water
1/4 pound ground lean pork
  butt
1 slice ginger root
1/2 teaspoon salt
1/4 cup diced water
  chestnuts
2 bunches watercress, large
  stems removed and coarsely
  chopped (1 quart loosely
  packed)
1 cup diced soybean curd

Bring water to boil, crumble in pork, and add ginger, salt and water chestnuts. Cook at gentle boil 15 minutes. Bring to hard boil, add watercress and cook 2 minutes. Add soybean curd and cook 3 minutes.

LOTUS ROOT SOUP

Serves 8 to 10

4 jujubes*, softened in water
  to cover
8 cups Basic Chinese Chicken
  or Pork Broth (page 105)
1 strand dried turnip green*,
  well washed (optional)
5 or 6 dried lotus roots*,
  soaked in water to cover 2
  hours and halved or quartered, or 1 pound fresh
  lotus roots, scraped and
  sliced
1 dried tangerine peel*,
  softened in water to cover
  10 minutes
4 to 6 dried forest mush-
  rooms, softened in water to
  cover and slivered
*See glossary

Slice jujubes, discarding pit;
combine with rest of ingredients, cover, bring to boil,
lower heat and simmer gently
2 hours. Remove tangerine
peel and turnip green before
serving.

SEAWEED SOUP

Serves 6 to 8

8 cups Basic Chinese Chicken
  or Pork Broth (page 105)
4 dried forest mushrooms,
  softened in water to cover
  and slivered
1 slice ginger root
1/4 cup dried shrimp*
1 handful of dried, bulk seaweed, soaked in water to
  cover 10 minutes, washed
  in 3 or 4 changes of
  water and coarsely chopped
1/2 cup ground pork
1/4 cup diced water chestnuts
1/4 cup chopped green onions
*See glossary

Combine broth, mushrooms,
ginger and shrimp; cover,
bring to boil, lower heat and
simmer 20 minutes. Add seaweed, pork and water chestnuts, bring to boil, lower heat
and simmer 15 minutes.
  Just before serving sprinkle
with green onions.

NOTE Six sheets of seaweed
(nori) may be substituted for
the bulk seaweed, but bulk is
tastier and has a better texture.

VARIATIONS Beat in 1 egg,
beaten, at last minute; or add
1 cup diced soybean curd
or 1/2 cup diced raw shrimp;
bring just to boil.

GAME BROTH

Serves 6

6 cups game broth
12 Chicken Balls or Force-
  meat Balls, cooked
  (page 171)
Minced fresh chervil
Parmesan croutons
6 tablespoons dry red wine

Heat broth to boil and adjust
seasonings.
  Add balls and garnish with
chervil and Parmesan croutons.
  Put 1 tablespoon of red
wine in each bowl and ladle
in hot broth.

SPAETZLE-SUPPE

Serves 6
6 cups broth of choice
Mixed minced fresh herbs

SPAETZLE
1 egg, beaten
1/2 cup milk
1 teaspoon butter, melted
1/2 teaspoon salt
5 tablespoons unbleached
  flour

To make spaetzle, combine egg, milk, butter and salt. Beat in flour. Bring broth to a boil. Force spaetzle mixture through a colander or spaetzle spoon into gently boiling broth. Cook 3 minutes until spaetzle rise to top. Simmer 3 more minutes. Sprinkle with herbs.

Take advantage of the new vegetable, soy and cornmeal pastas, in a variety of shapes, that are available in health-food stores.

BROTH WITH MACARONI

Serves 6
6 cups broth of choice
1/2 cup small shell macaroni
2 eggs, beaten with tiny bits
  of meat, liver, chicken or
  game and 1 teaspoon
  minced fresh parsley

Bring broth to boil, add macaroni and cook until al dente. Gradually drizzle egg mixture into gently broiling broth and cook until set.

BEEF BROTH WITH DUMPLINGS

Serves 6
5 cups beef broth
1 cup dry red wine
1/2 teaspoon sugar
1/2 tablespoon fresh lemon
  juice
1 recipe dumplings of choice,
  cooked (pages 169 to 171)
Lemon slices

Heat broth, wine, sugar and lemon juice and adjust to taste.
 Add cooked dumplings and serve with lemon slices.

VARIATION Omit wine and season 6 cups broth with minced fresh tarragon and/or oregano. Garnish with diced tomato.

TOMATO BOUILLON

Serves 6
4 cups chicken stock
2 cups chopped ripe tomatoes
Curry powder
Fresh lemon juice
Pinch sugar
1 recipe Marrow Dumplings,
  cooked (page 170)

Simmer stock and tomatoes 30 minutes. Force through food mill or sieve, reheat and season to taste with curry powder, lemon juice and sugar.
 Add dumplings and serve immediately.

PELMENY BROTH

Serves 4 to 6
6 cups broth of choice
1 recipe Pelmeny (following)
Minced fresh chives
Prepared hot mustard
White vinegar
Aji oil*
*See glossary

Bring broth to boil. Adjust seasoning. Divide cooked pelmeny among 4 to 6 bowls and ladle broth over them. Sprinkle with chives and pass hot mustard, white vinegar and aji oil.

PELMENY

DOUGH
1 cup sifted unbleached
  flour
1/2 teaspoon salt
1/4 cup water
2 egg yolks

FILLING
1 pound ground lean beef or
  combination of beef, pork
  and veal
3 tablespoons grated onion
1/2 teaspoon salt
1/4 teaspoon black pepper
1/4 cup minced mushrooms
1/2 teaspoon dill weed

Mix together dough ingredients and knead at least 10 minutes until smooth and elastic. Form into a ball and cover with inverted bowl for 1 hour. Roll into a rope 1/2 inch in diameter and cut into 1-inch lengths. Roll out each piece into a thin circle 2-1/2 inches in diameter.

Combine all filling ingredients. Put 3/4 teaspoon filling in the center of each round. Fold over to make half-moon shape and crimp edges to seal. Place on floured baking sheets and chill (or freeze) 30 minutes.

Cook in boiling salted water 7 minutes.

NOTE Ready-made round wonton skins may be used in place of homemade pelmeny skins.

CHICKEN-CLAM BROTH WITH ROYALES

Serves 6
5 cups chicken broth
1 cup clam juice
6 teaspoons dry sherry
1 recipe Royales (page 168)
Minced fresh chives
Paprika

Heat broth and clam juice; adjust seasonings to taste. Put a teaspoon of sherry in each of 6 heated bowls. Divide Royales among the bowls. Ladle in hot broth and sprinkle with chives and paprika.

VARIATION Float a curl of spinach leaf in each bowl with a shred of carrot and a tiny lemon peel.

Vegetable and Grain Soups

An idealist is one who, on noticing that a rose smells better than a cabbage, concludes it will also make better soup.

—H. L. Mencken

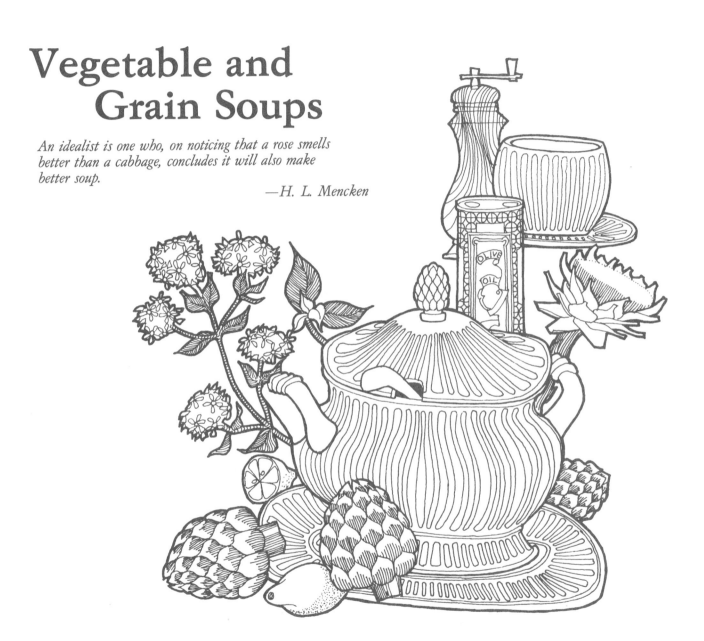

Fresh Vegetable Soups

ARTICHOKE SOUP

Serves 4 to 6

1 large garlic clove, minced
1/2 cup chopped onion
1 tablespoon olive oil
3 or 4 medium to large
  artichokes
3 cups broth of choice
  or as needed
1 tablespoon fresh lemon
  juice
1/2 teaspoon black pepper
4 sprigs oregano

4 green onions, chopped
  (white only)
1 large garlic clove, minced
6 ounces mushrooms, minced

2 tablespoons butter
1/4 cup creamy mushroom
  concentrate (page 14)
1 cup half-and-half cream
1/2 teaspoon *each* salt and
  white pepper
1/2 cup dry white wine

In large kettle, sauté garlic and onion in oil until translucent. Add artichokes, broth, lemon juice, pepper and oregano and simmer, covered, until artichokes are very tender, adding more broth if needed. Remove artichokes; strain and reserve broth.

Scrape edible portion from the artichoke leaves, remove and discard chokes and dice hearts, reserving 1 heart. Dice this heart and reserve it for garnish.

Sauté green onions, garlic and mushrooms in butter 3 minutes; purée with artichokes and 1 cup of the reserved broth. Combine purée with creamy mushroom concentrate and remaining broth. Heat, stirring, until smooth and slightly thickened. Add cream, salt and pepper.

Reheat and adjust seasonings. Just before serving, add wine and reserved diced artichoke heart.

VARIATION Add 1/4 cup tomato juice or to taste with cream.

Do not boil soups after adding cream or sour cream!

ASPARAGUS SOUP

Serves 4 to 6

1 pound asparagus, tough
  ends removed
2 cups loosely packed
  chopped red-leaf, escarole
  or any soft-leaf lettuce
4 green onions, chopped
  (white and some green)
1 garlic clove, minced
1 tablespoon minced fresh
  tarragon
2 tablespoons butter and/or
  rendered chicken fat
3 tablespoons rice flour
5 cups brown chicken stock
1/2 teaspoon salt
1/4 teaspoon black pepper
1/2 cup heavy cream
2 teaspoons fresh lemon juice
Minced fresh parsley and/or
  chives
Paprika

Cut tips from asparagus and
set aside. Cut stalks into 1-
inch pieces and sauté with
lettuce, onions, garlic and
tarragon in butter until soft
and lightly browned. Sprinkle
with flour and cook, stirring,
2 minutes. Stir in stock and
cook until slightly thickened,
then season with salt and
pepper.

Cover, bring to gentle boil,
lower heat and simmer 30
minutes, or until asparagus is
very soft. Purée and reheat
with cream; do not boil. Add
lemon juice and adjust seasonings with salt and pepper.
Garnish with parsley and
paprika.

BELL PEPPER SOUP

Serves 6

2 cups finely minced bell
  pepper
1 cup minced onions
1/4 cup minced carrot
1 garlic clove, minced
3 slices bacon, minced
2 cups peeled and chopped
  ripe tomatoes
4 cups beef and/or chicken
  stock
1/2 teaspoon salt
1/4 teaspoon black pepper
1/2 teaspoon minced fresh
  basil
1 pound ground round steak

Sauté bell pepper, onion, carrot, garlic and bacon until
bacon is slightly browned.
Add tomatoes, stock, salt,
pepper, basil and meat. Cover, bring to boil, lower heat
and simmer 45 minutes. Adjust seasonings to taste. Serve
with garlic French bread.

CREAMY
BELL PEPPER SOUP

Serves 4 to 6

1 cup diced bell pepper
1/2 cup diced onion
1 garlic clove, minced
2 tablespoons butter and/or
  rendered chicken fat
2 tablespoons unbleached
  flour
1/4 teaspoon crumbled dried
  marjoram
3 cups chicken stock
1-1/2 cups milk and/or half-
  and-half cream
1/8 teaspoon white pepper
1/2 teaspoon freshly grated
  lemon peel
Salt
Bell pepper, sliced paper thin
  and/or lemon slices

---

*Bell peppers vary in strength
and flavor. Taste first!*

Sauté bell pepper, onion and garlic in butter until soft. Sprinkle with flour and marjoram; cook, stirring, 3 minutes. Gradually add stock, cook and stir until smooth and slightly thickened, cover and simmer gently 30 minutes.

Purée, add milk and season with pepper and lemon peel. Reheat and adjust seasonings with salt; or chill and adjust seasonings.

Garnish with bell pepper slices.

CREAM OF BROCCOLI SOUP

Serves 6 to 8

2 to 2-1/2 pounds broccoli
1/2 cup chopped onion
1/4 cup minced bell pepper
1 rib celery, chopped
2 tablespoons butter and/or
    rendered chicken fat
2 tablespoons unbleached
    flour
6 cups brown chicken stock

Bouquet garni of
    1 bay leaf
    3 sprigs parsley
    1 sprig thyme
    6 black peppercorns,
      lightly crushed
1/4 teaspoon freshly grated
    nutmeg
1/4 teaspoon white pepper
2 or 3 egg yolks
1 cup heavy cream or half-
    and-half cream
Salt to taste
Slivered green onions
Sour cream

Reserve 12 small broccoli flowerets and chop remainder. Sauté chopped broccoli, onion and bell pepper in butter to brown slightly.

Sprinkle with flour, cook, stirring, 3 minutes, and add stock and bouquet garni. Cook and stir until smooth and

---

Lettuce sat in the refrigerator too long? Shred it, cook in a little butter and add to soup before puréeing it.

---

slightly thickened. Cover, bring to boil, lower heat and simmer 30 minutes, or until broccoli is soft. Discard bouquet garni.

Purée and force through sieve to remove any stringy particles. Add nutmeg and pepper.

Beat together yolks and cream, whisk in 1/2 cup hot soup and return to rest of soup. Reheat; do not boil. Season with salt and serve with slivered green onions and dollops of sour cream.

VARIATIONS Omit nutmeg. Add 2 tablespoons tomato paste with pepper and mix well. After adding egg yolks and cream, reheat with 1 cup cooked macaroni and serve garnished with freshly grated Parmesan cheese.

Add 2 ripe tomatoes, peeled and chopped, after adding cream and egg yolks. Garnish with toasted slivered almonds.

CREAMY CABBAGE SOUP

Serves 6 to 8
1/4 cup minced salt pork
2 tablespoons unsalted butter
3 tablespoons minced shallots
1 garlic clove, minced
1 tablespoon unbleached flour
5 cups chicken or beef stock
4 cups finely shredded Savoy
  cabbage

Bouquet garni of
  1 bay leaf
  2 sprigs parsley
  1 sprig thyme
  6 black peppercorns,
    lightly crushed

1 cup half-and-half cream or
  milk
3/4 cup sour cream
1/8 teaspoon freshly grated
  nutmeg
1/4 teaspoon white pepper
1/2 teaspoon salt
2 egg yolks, beaten
1/2 cup heavy cream
Minced fresh parsley
Freshly grated Swiss cheese

Brown salt pork in butter,
remove with slotted spoon
and reserve.

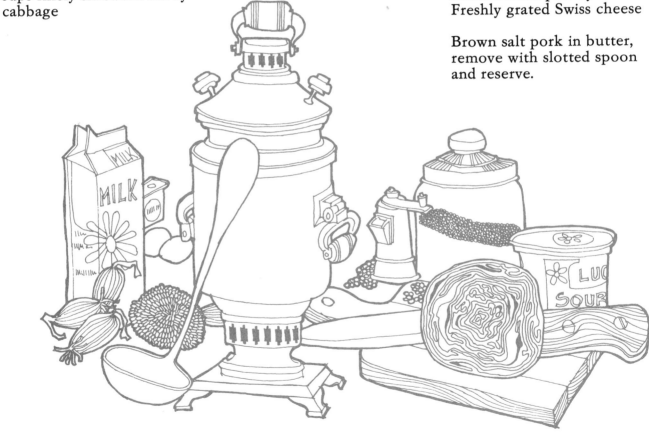

Add shallots and garlic to pan and sauté until just golden. Sprinkle with flour, cook, stirring, 3 minutes and gradually add stock. Cook and stir until smooth and slightly thickened. Add cabbage and bouquet garni, cover, bring to boil, lower heat and simmer 30 minutes. Discard bouquet garni and purée soup. Mix together half-and-half cream and sour cream, stir into purée and reheat.

Season with nutmeg, pepper and salt. Beat together yolks and heavy cream, whisk in 1/2 cup soup and return to rest of soup. Reheat without boiling; adjust seasoning with salt.

Garnish with reheated salt pork bits, parsley and Swiss cheese.

VARIATIONS Add peeled and chopped ripe tomatoes or sautéed minced bell pepper and julienne of ham after adding yolks and cream.

CARROT PUREE

Serves 6

1-1/2 pounds carrots, sliced (4 cups)
1 rib celery, chopped (1 cup)
2 cups chopped leeks (white and some green)
1/2-inch piece bay leaf
6 sprigs parsley
6 cups chicken stock
1 cup half-and-half cream
3 tablespoons butter
1/8 teaspoon freshly grated nutmeg
1/4 teaspoon white pepper
1/2 teaspoon freshly grated lemon peel
1/2 teaspoon brown sugar
1/2 cup coarsely grated carrot
1/4 cup heavy cream
Salt
Minced fresh parsley or mint
Croutons or toast rounds

Cook sliced carrots, celery, leeks, bay leaf and parsley in 1 cup of the stock, covered, until very soft. Remove bay leaf and purée, using more stock if needed. Force through fine sieve, add rest of stock, half-and-half cream, butter and seasonings. Heat, but do not boil.

Melt brown sugar in saucepan and cook, stirring, 3 to 4 minutes. Add grated carrot and heavy cream, cover and cook 5 minutes, or until carrot is tender-crisp. Add to hot soup, adjust seasonings, adding salt as needed, and sprinkle with parsley. Pass the croutons.

VARIATIONS Garnish with grated onion, or float tiny balls of Gorgonzola cheese rolled in paprika on top.

Heavy cream is salty, so wait to adjust seasoning until after it is added.

CARROT-ORANGE SOUP

Serves 4 to 6
1 small leek, thinly sliced
   (white and some green)
1/4 cup chopped onion
4 sprigs parsley, coarsely
   chopped
2 large carrots, sliced
1 teaspoon fresh thyme leaves
2 tablespoons butter and/or
   rendered chicken fat
4 cups chicken stock
2/3 cup fresh orange juice
3 tablespoons sour cream
1/4 teaspoon ground ginger,
   or to taste
Salt and white pepper to taste
Sour cream
Minced fresh parsley and/or
   chives

Lightly brown leek, onion,
parsley, carrots and thyme in
butter. Add stock, bring to
gentle boil, cover, lower heat
and simmer 20 minutes or
until carrots are soft.

   Purée and reheat with orange
juice, sour cream and seasonings. Adjust to taste and garnish with dollops of sour
cream and minced parsley.

CAULIFLOWER SOUP WITH CHEESE

Serves 6
4 cups cauliflowerets
4 cups chicken stock
1 teaspoon soy sauce
1/2 teaspoon crumbled dried
   savory
1/2 teaspoon paprika
1 garlic clove, minced
1/4 teaspoon black pepper
2 tablespoons butter
2 tablespoons unbleached
   flour
1 cup evaporated milk
1/4 cup freshly grated
   Parmesan or Romano cheese
2 egg yolks, beaten
3 tablespoons fresh lemon
juice
Additional grated cheese

Reserve 1/2 cup tiny cauliflowerets for garnish. Cook
remainder in stock with soy
sauce, savory, paprika, garlic
and pepper until cauliflower
is soft. Purée.

   Melt butter until bubbly,
add flour, and cook, stirring,
3 minutes. Gradually add
milk; cook and stir until
thickened and add purée and
cheese. Reheat to melt cheese.

Beat eggs with lemon juice,
whisk in 1/2 cup hot soup
and return to rest of soup.
Reheat; do not boil.

   Garnish with reserved raw
flowerets and extra cheese.

CREAM OF CELERY ROOT SOUP

Serves 4
1-1/2 cups diced celery root
1/2 cup diced onion
2 tablespoons minced leeks
   (white part only)
1 teaspoon minced garlic
3 tablespoons butter
1/2 teaspoon dry mustard
1/8 teaspoon sugar
2 cups chicken or veal stock
1 cup half-and-half cream or
   milk
Salt, white pepper, celery
   salt and freshly grated
   lemon peel
3/4 cup tiny celery root
   julienne, raw or cooked in
   a little stock until just
   tender
Paprika
Minced fresh parsley

Sauté celery root, onion, leeks and garlic in butter 5 minutes. Sprinkle with mustard and sugar and cook and stir 5 more minutes.

Add stock, cover, bring to boil, lower heat and simmer until celery root is tender. Purée, add cream and reheat without boiling. Season to taste with salt, pepper, celery salt and lemon peel.

Serve garnished with celery root julienne and a sprinkling of paprika and parsley.

VARIATION This soup may also be served cold. Chill, adjust seasonings and serve in chilled bowls garnished with tiny lemon peel strips.

CREAM OF CELERY SOUP

Serves 4 to 6
2 cups chopped celery and some leaves
1 cup chopped onions
4 cups brown chicken stock
2 cups diagonally sliced celery
1/2 cup chopped celery leaves
3 tablespoons butter
3 tablespoons unbleached flour
2 cups half-and-half cream or milk
1/8 teaspoon freshly grated nutmeg
1/4 teaspoon white pepper
1/2 teaspoon celery salt
Salt to taste
Chiffonade of sorrel (page 172)
Lemon slices

Simmer chopped celery and onion in stock, covered, 45 minutes. Strain.

Sauté sliced celery and leaves in butter 5 minutes, sprinkle with flour and cook, stirring, 3 minutes. Gradually add stock; cook and stir until smooth and slightly thickened.

Cover and simmer 15 minutes. Add cream and seasonings and reheat. Adjust seasonings with salt.

Just before serving stir in chiffonade of sorrel and garnish with lemon slices.

VARIATION Add 2 tomatoes, peeled, seeded and diced, when simmering thickened soup. Garnish with bacon bits or toasted slivered unblanched almonds and minced fresh parsley or top with freshly grated cheese.

CUCUMBER-CELERY SOUP

Serves 4

3 cucumbers, peeled, seeded
  and cut into 1-inch julienne
2 ribs celery, thinly sliced on
  diagonal
1 leek, minced (white only)
1 teaspoon minced fresh
  thyme
1/4 cup minced fresh parsley
1/4 teaspoon black pepper
2 tablespoons butter
1-1/2 tablespoons unbleached
  flour
3-1/2 cups brown chicken
  stock
1/4 cup dry white wine
1/4 teaspoon salt
1 egg yolk, beaten
1 cup heavy cream or half-
  and-half cream
1/2 teaspoon fresh lemon juice
1/4 teaspoon *each* white
  pepper and celery salt
Lemon slices
Parsley sprigs

Cook 1 of the cucumbers, celery, leek and herbs in butter, covered, until vegetables are soft.

Sprinkle with flour, cook, stirring, 3 minutes, then gradually add stock and wine. Cook and stir until smooth and slightly thickened. Cover and simmer 10 minutes.

While soup is simmering, sprinkle remaining cucumbers with salt and let stand in colander to drain. Rinse, drain and dry on paper toweling. Add to soup and cook 4 minutes.

Beat together yolk and cream, whisk in 1/2 cup hot soup and return to rest of soup. Reheat, but do not boil. Season with lemon juice, pepper and celery salt and adjust to taste. Serve garnished with lemon slices and tiny parsley sprigs.

VARIATION Add a chiffonade of sorrel (page 172) in place of the lemon slices and serve with lemon croutons.

CURRIED EGGPLANT SOUP

Serves 3 or 4
1 cup cubed unpeeled
 eggplant
1 tablespoon olive oil
1/4 cup minced green onions
 and tops
1/2 teaspoon minced garlic
1 tablespoon butter
4 teaspoons unbleached flour
1 to 2 teaspoons curry powder
2 cups milk
1 sprig rosemary
2 sprigs oregano
1/2 cup heavy cream
Salt and black pepper to taste

Sauté eggplant in oil until golden. In saucepan, sauté onions and garlic in butter until onions are soft. Sprinkle with flour and curry powder, cook, stirring, 3 minutes and gradually add milk. Cook and stir until thickened, then add rosemary, oregano and eggplant. Simmer 15 minutes. Force through sieve, discarding eggplant peel and herb stems.

Heat, add cream and reheat; do not boil. Adjust seasonings with salt and pepper.

GREEN SOUP

Serves 4 to 6
1/2 cup *each* finely chopped
 sorrel, spinach, dandelion
 greens, kale, Swiss chard or
 any green leafy vegetable
 or combination to make 2
 to 3 cups
1 rib celery, thinly sliced on
 diagonal
1/2 cup minced green onions
 (white and some green)
1/4 cup *each* minced leek
 (white only), fresh parsley
 and watercress
3 tablespoons butter
1 tablespoon unbleached flour
4 cups brown chicken stock
1 cup sour cream
1/2 teaspoon salt
1/4 teaspoon black pepper
1 tablespoon fresh lemon
 juice
Paprika
Toast fingers

Sauté vegetables, parsley and watercress in butter until well coated and wilted. Sprinkle with flour, cook, stirring, 3 minutes, then gradually add stock. Cook and stir until smooth. Cover, bring to boil, lower heat and simmer gently until celery is just tender-crisp.

Remove from heat, mix sour cream into 1/2 cup of hot soup and then return to rest of soup. Season and adjust to taste. Sprinkle with paprika and serve with toast fingers.

VARIATION Add little force-meat balls of game (page 171). Garnish with thinly sliced radishes.

Unless the soup is to be puréed, always cook vegetables until they are barely tender. They should remain crisp.

ITALIAN GREEN BEAN AND FENNEL PUREE

Serves 4 to 6
1/2 cup chopped onion and/ or white of leek
1 garlic clove, minced
2 tablespoons rendered chicken fat and/or butter
3 cups cut-up Italian green beans
1/2 to 1 teaspoon fennel seeds
5 cups brown chicken stock
1/2 cup *each* milk and half-and-half cream
1/2 cup sour cream, or to taste
Salt and white pepper to taste
Finely chopped fresh fennel feathers, parsley and/or chives

Lightly brown onion and garlic in chicken fat. Add beans and fennel seeds, stir to coat and add stock. Cover, bring to gentle boil, lower heat and simmer 15 minutes or until beans are softened. Purée, sieve and reheat with milk, cream and sour cream. Season with salt and pepper. Garnish with fennel feathers.

LEEK-TOMATO SOUP

Serves 4 to 6
2 large leeks, chopped (white and some green)
2 tablespoons butter
4 cups peeled and chopped ripe tomatoes
1 bay leaf
4 basil leaves
1 sprig tarragon
1/4 teaspoon *each* salt and black pepper
Pinch sugar
1/3 cup orzo, cooked al dente
Chicken or beef stock (optional)
Half-and-half cream (optional)
1 large tomato, peeled and diced
Minced fresh chives

Sauté leeks in butter until soft. Add chopped tomatoes, herbs and seasonings. Cover, bring to gentle boil, lower heat and simmer 30 minutes. Discard bay leaf and purée. Reheat with orzo and stock or cream if thinner soup is desired.
  Adjust seasonings and garnish with diced tomato and chives.

VARIATION For a heartier meal, add crumbled cooked ground beef or veal, cooked corn kernels, peas, beans.

BROCCOLI-MUSHROOM SOUP

Serves 4 to 6
3 to 4 ounces salt pork or bacon, diced
1 leek, thinly sliced (white only)
1 medium onion, thinly sliced
2 garlic cloves, minced
Butter
4 to 5 ounces mushrooms, sliced
1 teaspoon minced fresh oregano
Dash cayenne pepper
2 to 3 cups broccoli purée
4 to 5 cups brown chicken stock
1 or 2 potatoes, scrubbed and sliced
1 or 2 tomatoes, peeled and chopped
Diced cooked chicken, turkey or ham (optional)
Salt and white pepper to taste
Minced fresh parsley and/or chives
Paprika

In heavy saucepan, brown salt pork, remove with slotted spoon and set aside. Add leek, onion and garlic, cover and steam until onion is translucent, adding butter if needed. Remove lid, add mushrooms and sauté until lightly golden, sprinkling with oregano and cayenne while cooking. Remove with slotted spoon and set aside.

Add broccoli purée, stock, potatoes and tomatoes. Cover, bring to gentle boil, lower heat and simmer until potatoes are just tender. Add chicken, reserved salt pork, mushroom mixture and salt and pepper and heat through. Serve, generously sprinkled with minced parsley and paprika.

TOMATO-MUSHROOM SOUP

Serves 4 to 6
1 leek, chopped (white only)
2 ribs celery and some leaves, chopped
1 large garlic clove, minced
2 tablespoons butter and/or rendered chicken fat
10 ounces mushrooms
4 cups peeled and chopped ripe tomatoes
2 cups brown chicken stock
1/2 cup dry vermouth
1 teaspoon tomato paste
1/2 teaspoon salt
1/4 teaspoon black pepper
1/8 teaspoon sugar
Bouquet garni of
    3 sprigs parsley
    2 sprigs dill
    2 sprigs thyme or lemon thyme
    2 sprigs oregano
    4 basil leaves
    1 bay leaf
1/2 cup chopped watercress leaves
1/2 cup heavy cream (optional)
Minced fresh chives

Sauté leek, celery and garlic in butter until softened. Dice 8 ounces of the mushrooms and add, cooking quickly to brown slightly. Add tomatoes, stock, vermouth, tomato paste and seasonings. Stir well, add bouquet garni, cover, bring to gentle boil, lower heat and simmer 30 minutes. Discard bouquet garni and purée.

Finely mince remaining mushrooms, add to soup and boil gently 10 minutes. Add watercress and boil gently 3 minutes. Add cream, if desired, heat without boiling and adjust seasonings. Garnish with chives.

Recipe calls for 1 teaspoon tomato paste? Try buying tomato paste in a tube rather than opening a can and having to worry about using up the rest right away.

EMMA'S MUSHROOM SOUP

For years Emma ruled the kitchen of a family who ate well, indeed. Now, years later, her original recipe can still hold its own against those of famous chefs.

Serves 4 to 6

1 pound round steak, cut into 1-inch cubes
1 teaspoon salt
4-1/2 cups water
1/2 cup minced onion
4 tablespoons butter, or as needed
1 pound mushrooms, minced
2-1/2 tablespoons unbleached flour

1 cup half-and-half cream
Salt
Paprika
Minced fresh parsley

Sprinkle meat with salt, add cold water and let stand 1/2 hour. Cover, bring to slow boil, lower heat and simmer gently until meat is tender. Remove meat and reserve for another use. Do not strain as the flavor of the "curds" that have formed enhances the soup. Set broth aside.

Sauté onion in butter until soft but not brown. Add mushrooms and sauté 5 minutes; sprinkle with flour, cook, stirring, 3 minutes, then gradually add reserved broth. Cook and stir until slightly thickened.

Add cream and reheat; do not boil. Season with salt and serve sprinkled with paprika and parsley.

VARIATION Garnish with dollops of whipped cream.

SPINACH SOUP

Serves 6

1 pound fresh spinach, chopped (6 to 7 cups, loosely packed)
2 tablespoons minced green onion
1 garlic clove, minced
3 tablespoons butter
1/8 teaspoon freshly grated nutmeg
5 cups chicken, beef or veal stock
1 cup half-and-half cream
Pinch sugar
1/2 teaspoon salt
1/4 teaspoon white pepper
Fresh lemon juice to taste
Butter, cut into bits
Sieved hard-cooked eggs
Paprika

Sauté spinach, green onion and garlic in butter, stirring, until spinach is wilted.

Add nutmeg and stock, cover, bring to boil, lower heat and simmer 20 minutes. Purée.

Add cream and seasonings, heat and adjust to taste. Swirl in butter and sprinkle with sieved hard-cooked eggs and paprika.

VARIATION Halve 3 small hard-cooked eggs, remove yolks and mash them with 1-1/2 teaspoons softened butter. Form balls and arrange in white halves. Garnish with a tiny parsley sprig, and float on hot soup.

SORREL AND LETTUCE SOUP

Serves 4

1 rib celery, very thinly sliced on the diagonal (1/2 cup)
1/2 teaspoon finely minced garlic
1-1/2 tablespoons rendered chicken fat or butter
3 ounces sorrel, stems and tough ribs removed, shredded (2 cups)
2 cups loosely packed shredded red-leaf or other soft-leaf lettuce
3 tablespoons minced fresh chives
Pinch sugar
4 cups brown chicken or veal stock
Salt, white pepper and fresh lemon juice to taste
1 egg, lightly beaten
Chopped celery leaves or sour cream

Cook celery and garlic in butter, covered, until almost tender. Add sorrel, lettuce, chives and sugar. Stir well to coat sorrel and lettuce and cook, stirring, 3 minutes. Add stock, cover, bring to gentle boil and cook 4 minutes. Season with salt, pepper and lemon juice. Bring to boil and with fork beat in egg, stirring until set. Garnish with celery leaves or dollops of sour cream.

SUNCHOKE-SORREL PUREE

Serves 4

4 ounces unpeeled sunchokes, chopped (approximately 1-1/2 cups)
3 to 4 ounces sorrel, stems and tough ribs removed, shredded (2 cups)
1/4 cup minced onion
1 teaspoon minced garlic
2 tablespoons rendered chicken fat and/or butter
4 cups brown chicken stock
Salt and white pepper to taste
Minced fresh chives or green onion tops

Cook sunchokes, sorrel, onion and garlic in chicken fat, covered, 10 minutes. Add stock, cover, bring to gentle boil, lower heat and simmer 20 minutes or until sunchokes are soft. Purée, reheat and season with salt and pepper. Garnish with chives.

MIXED ROOT VEGETABLE PUREE WITH BARLEY

Serves 6 to 8

1 large carrot, chopped
1 parsnip, chopped
1 large leek, chopped (white and some green)
1 onion, chopped
1 small celery root, chopped
4 sprigs parsley, including tender stems, chopped
3 tablespoons butter and/or rendered chicken fat
6 to 8 cups brown chicken stock
1/2 cup hulled barley
Fresh lemon juice, salt and white pepper to taste

Sliced mushrooms, rubbed
  with fresh lemon juice, or
  shredded raw carrots or
  celery root, or julienned
  red and/or green bell pepper
Minced fresh parsley

Lightly brown vegetables and
parsley in butter. Add barley
and cook, stirring, several
minutes. Add 3 cups of the
stock, cover, bring to gentle
boil, lower heat and simmer
30 minutes or until barley is
barely tender. Cool slightly
and purée. Add remaining
stock, reheat and season with
lemon juice, salt and pepper.
Serve garnished with raw vegetables and parsley.

VARIATION Substitute milk and/
or half-and-half cream for a
portion of the stock. Heat
without boiling.

QUICK PARSNIP CHOWDER

For each serving
1 slice lean bacon, diced
1 small parsnip, lightly
  scraped and diced
1 small new red potato,
  scrubbed and diced
2 tablespoons chopped onion
2 to 3 tablespoons stock
1 cup low-fat milk, milk
  and/or half-and-half cream
Salt and white pepper to taste
Minced fresh parsley
Paprika

Cook bacon until crisp. Remove with slotted spoon and
set aside. Brown parsnip, potato and onion in bacon drippings, add stock, cover tightly
and cook gently until vegetables are just tender. Add
milk, heat without boiling
and adjust seasonings with
salt and pepper. Garnish with
reserved bacon, parsley and
paprika.

SWEET POTATO SOUP

Serves 6
1 cup chopped onions
3 ribs celery, chopped
1 pound sweet potatoes or
  yams, peeled and sliced
1 tablespoon bacon fat
6 cups chicken stock
1/4 cup minced fresh parsley
Salt, black pepper and freshly
  grated nutmeg to taste
Sour cream

Cook onions, celery and sweet
potatoes in bacon fat, covered
and stirring often, 5 minutes.
Add stock, cover, bring to
boil, lower heat and simmer
until soft.
  Purée, add parsley and reheat. Season with salt, pepper
and nutmeg. Pass a bowl of
sour cream.

Potato Soups

Russet, or baking potatoes, are the best type to use for making potato soups. Scrub them well and peel, if desired. If you do peel them, reserve the skins for making stocks.

HOT POTATO SOUP

Serves 6
1-1/2 cups minced leeks
 (white and some green)
1/4 cup minced onion
1 large garlic clove, minced
3 tablespoons minced carrot
4 tablespoons butter and/or
 rendered chicken fat
4 cups brown chicken stock
1-1/2 cups diced potatoes
1/2 cup heavy cream
Salt, white pepper and Beau
 Monde seasoning to taste
Additional chicken stock or
 half-and-half cream, if
 needed

Sauté leeks, onion, garlic and carrot in butter until leeks are soft. Do not brown.
 Add stock and potatoes, cover, bring to boil, lower heat and simmer until pota-

toes are tender. Purée. Add cream and reheat, but do not boil. Season with salt, pepper and Beau Monde. If too thick, thin with more stock or with half-and-half cream.

VARIATION Just before serving, add 3 tablespoons dry vermouth or dry sherry. Or sprinkle with caraway seeds.

BROCCOLI-POTATO

Serves 6
1 recipe Hot Potato Soup
  without cream
1-1/2 cups cooked chopped
  broccoli
1-1/2 tablespoons grated
  onion
1 cup half-and-half cream
Minced fresh dill or tiny raw
  broccoli flowerets

Prepare potato soup and combine with broccoli and onion. Simmer 10 minutes to blend flavors. Purée.
  Reheat with cream and adjust seasonings to taste. Garnish with minced dill.

VARIATION Add 1/2 cup heavy cream and chill. Serve with tiny cooked shrimp.

CARROT-POTATO

Serves 6
1 recipe Hot Potato Soup
  without cream
1 cup diced carrots
1/4 cup diced celery
3 tablespoons butter
1 teaspoon minced fresh
  marjoram
Pinch sugar
1/2 cup grated carrot
1 cup half-and-half cream
Salt, white pepper and
  minced fresh marjoram
  to taste
Minced fresh parsley

Prepare potato soup and set aside.
  Sauté diced carrots and celery in butter until soft, sprinkling with marjoram and sugar as they are cooking. Purée with some of the potato soup, combine with rest of soup, add grated carrot and simmer 5 minutes.
  Reheat with cream and adjust seasonings to taste with salt, pepper and marjoram. Sprinkle with a generous amount of parsley.

Save potato peelings and add to stock pot for extra nutrients.

VARIATION Add 1/2 cup heavy cream, chill and garnish with grated raw carrot and minced fresh parsley.

CUCUMBER-POTATO

Serves 6
1 recipe Hot Potato Soup
  without cream
1 large cucumber, peeled,
  seeded and grated
3 tablespoons grated onion
1 cup half-and-half cream
Salt, white pepper and fresh
  lemon juice to taste
Freshly grated lemon peel
Minced fresh dill, slivered
  green onions or finely
  minced sweet pickle

Prepare potato soup and combine with cucumber and onion; simmer 10 minutes. Reheat with cream, but do not boil. Adjust seasonings with salt, pepper and lemon juice. Sprinkle with lemon peel and dill.

VARIATION Add 1/2 cup heavy cream, chill and garnish with minced fresh mint and sour cream.

MUSHROOM-POTATO

Serves 6
1 recipe Hot Potato Soup
  without cream
1 cup finely minced
  mushrooms
1/4 cup *each* minced celery
  and green onions
3 tablespoons butter
1/4 teaspoon garlic powder
1/2 teaspoon fresh lemon juice

Dash ground oregano
1 cup half-and-half cream
Salt and black pepper to taste
Paprika
Minced fresh dill or parsley

Prepare potato soup and set aside.

Sauté mushrooms, celery and green onions in butter until soft, sprinkling with seasonings as they cook. Purée with some of the potato soup, combine with rest of soup, add cream and reheat, but do not boil. Adjust seasonings with salt and pepper.

Sprinkle with paprika and dill.

VARIATION Add 1/2 cup heavy cream, chill and garnish with dollops of sour cream and thinly sliced raw mushrooms that have been rubbed with lemon juice.

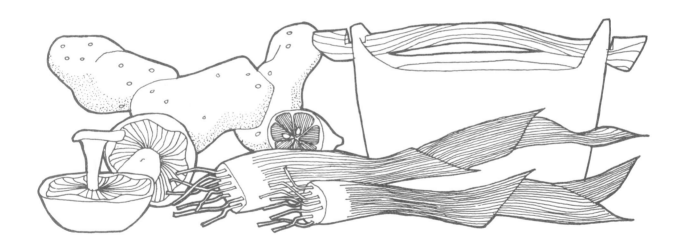

PARSLEY-POTATO

Serves 6
1 recipe Hot Potato Soup
  without cream
1 bunch parsley
1/4 cup diced celery
3 tablespoons butter
1 cup half-and-half cream
1 bunch parsley
Salt and white pepper to taste
Lemon croutons

Prepare potato soup and set aside.

Remove stems from parsley and mince; reserve the sprigs. Sauté celery and stems in butter until celery is soft. Purée with some of the potato soup, combine with rest of soup, cream and parsley sprigs and simmer 5 minutes.

Adjust seasonings with salt and pepper. Serve with lemon croutons.

VARIATION Add 1/2 cup heavy cream, chill and serve with a sprinkle of paprika.

PEA-POTATO

Serves 6
1 recipe Hot Potato Soup
  without cream
2-1/2 cups shelled green peas
1/4 cup minced celery
3 tablespoons butter
1 cup half-and-half cream
Salt, white pepper and minced
  fresh savory to taste
Butter, cut into bits
Paprika

Prepare potato soup and set aside.

Cook 1 cup of the peas and the celery in butter, covered, until soft.

Purée with some of the potato soup; combine with rest of soup, rest of peas and the cream. Simmer 5 minutes, but do not boil.

Adjust seasonings with salt, pepper and savory. Swirl in butter and sprinkle with paprika.

VARIATION Omit butter bits. Add 1/2 cup heavy cream, chill and serve with a garnish of minced fresh mint.

SORREL-POTATO

Serves 6
1 recipe Hot Potato Soup
  without cream
2 to 3 cups chopped sorrel
1 tablespoon butter and/or
  rendered chicken fat
1-1/2 cups half-and-half
  cream
2 egg yolks, beaten
Salt, white pepper, minced
  fresh herbs and freshly
  grated lemon peel to taste
Paprika

Prepare potato soup and set aside.

Cook sorrel, covered, in butter 10 minutes, stirring occasionally.

Combine with potato soup and heat. Beat together cream and egg yolks, whisk in 1/2 cup hot soup and return to rest of soup. Adjust seasonings with salt, pepper, herbs and lemon peel. Serve with a dusting of paprika.

VARIATION Add 1/2 cup heavy cream, chill and garnish with chervil.

WATERCRESS-POTATO

Serves 6
1 recipe Hot Potato Soup
   without cream
1 bunch watercress
1/4 cup diced celery
3 tablespoons butter
1 cup half-and-half cream
Salt and white pepper to taste
Garlic croutons

Prepare potato soup and set aside. Remove stems from watercress and mince; reserve the leaves. Sauté celery and the stems in butter until celery is soft. Purée with a little of the soup and combine with rest of soup, cream and watercress leaves. Simmer 5 minutes, adjust seasonings with salt and pepper, and serve with garlic croutons.

VARIATION Add 1/2 cup heavy cream, chill and garnish with extra watercress.

Legume Soups

HOW TO COOK DRIED LEGUMES

Cooking times for dried legumes vary according to age, size and type. Small ones, such as lentils and split peas, will cook in as little as 20 to 30 minutes, while larger or older ones may take one and a half hours or longer. Soaking them before cooking will shorten this time by as much as 30 minutes, making soaking of the small ones unnecessary.

There are two basic soaking methods. The first is to cover the legumes with water, using the ratio of two to three parts water to one part legumes, and let stand overnight. Do not soak them any longer than this or they may begin to ferment. If it is a hot day, put them in the refrigerator to soak to prevent them from souring. For the second method, place the legumes in a pot and add boiling water in the same proportion used in the first method. Bring to a boil and boil gently for two minutes. Remove from the heat and let stand, covered, for one to two hours.

Cook the beans in the water in which they were soaking, with the exception of soybeans, which sometimes turn the water bitter. Bring to a boil, lower the heat and boil gently with the lid tilted about one-eighth inch. The legumes are cooked when they are tender, but still retain their identity. However, if you intend to purée them, cook them until they are very soft.

You may add vegetables, such as a quartered onion, a garlic clove or a chili pepper, to the legumes while they are cooking to impart additional flavor. Most sources do not recommend adding salt to legumes until they are cooked because it draws out moisture.

If possible, purchase dried legumes at health-food or other bulk-food stores, as they tend to be fresher than when bought packaged at a supermarket. Buying at these stores also gives you the opportunity to control the amount you take home, so that dried legumes do not age on the kitchen shelf. One pound dried legumes measures approximately two cups, depending on size, and when cooked, they triple in volume. Store in airtight containers in a cool, dry place.

LENTIL SOUPS

Lentils, distinct in flavor and rich in protein and carbohydrates, have thrived in the light dry soil of Mediterranean countries since at least 2200 B.C., providing soups and cereal for man, and fodder for animals. Magnifying lenses, when invented, were named after lentils because of their similar, rounded, convex surfaces. Peas and beans may be more popular as table food in the United States, but lentils will always retain their importance as an ingredient of soup.

LENTIL SOUP

Serves 6
1 large ham hock, blanched and rinsed
4 cups water
2 cups chicken stock
1 bay leaf
1 whole onion, stuck with 3 whole cloves
2 carrots, thinly sliced
1 onion, thinly sliced
1 rib celery, thinly sliced on diagonal
2 garlic cloves, minced
2 tablespoons olive oil
1 cup dried brown lentils
2 cups peeled and chopped ripe tomatoes
Salt and white pepper
1/2 teaspoon crumbled dried Italian herbs
Minced fresh chives or freshly grated Parmesan cheese

Combine ham hock, water, stock, bay leaf and whole onion. Cover, bring to boil, lower heat and simmer 3 hours, or until ham hock is tender. Remove ham hock and set aside. Discard bay leaf and whole onion. Reserve cooking liquid.

Sauté carrot, sliced onion, celery and garlic in oil until lightly browned. Add lentils, stir to coat and mix in tomatoes, herbs and reserved cooking liquid. Cover, bring to boil, lower heat and simmer 30 minutes or until lentils are just tender. Remove meat from ham hocks, return meat to soup, reheat and adjust seasonings with salt, pepper and Italian herbs. Garnish with chives.

Many soups, such as lentil and oxtail, improve with reheating, so save time by making a day ahead.

BROWN LENTIL AND POTATO SOUP

Serves 4 to 6

1 cup dried brown lentils
6 cups beef stock
1/4 pound salt pork, diced
1/2 cup *each* diced carrot,
    onion and celery
Bouquet garni of
    1 orange, quartered
    3 whole cloves
    3 sprigs parsley
    1 bay leaf
    1 sprig thyme
    6 black peppercorns, lightly
      crushed
1/2 teaspoon salt
2 potatoes, scrubbed and
    diced
2 tablespoons butter and/or
    rendered pork or beef fat
2 tablespoons rice flour
Dry sherry
Sour cream
Slivered green onions

Combine lentils, stock, salt pork, vegetables, bouquet garni and salt. Cover, bring to boil, lower heat and simmer 30 minutes. Add potatoes and simmer 15 minutes. Discard bouquet garni.

Melt butter until bubbly, sprinkle with flour, and cook, stirring, 3 minutes. Gradually add soup and cook, stirring, until slightly thickened.

Put 1/2 tablespoon dry sherry in each bowl and ladle in soup. Top with several dollops of sour cream and a sprinkling of green onions.

VARIATION Reheat with chopped ripe tomatoes and cooked garlic sausages. Garnish with grated raw zucchini.

MASUR LENTIL SOUP WITH WINE

Serves 4 to 6
1/4 cup minced bacon or
    salt pork
1/2 cup minced onion
1/4 cup minced carrot
1/3 cup diced celery
2 tablespoons chopped fresh
    parsley
1 garlic clove, minced
1 teaspoon *each* chopped
    fresh oregano and summer
    savory
1/2 teaspoon salt
1/4 teaspoon black pepper
1 cup dried red lentils
1-1/2 cups Beef Consommé
    (page 20)
4 cups beef stock
1 cup tomato juice
1 to 2 tablespoons fresh
    lemon juice
1/3 cup dry red wine
Lemon slices
Minced fresh chives

Sauté bacon, vegetables, garlic, herbs and seasonings until bacon is browned. Add lentils, consommé and stock. Cover, bring to boil, lower heat and simmer 30 minutes or until lentils are soft. Purée, reheat with tomato juice and lemon juice and adjust seasonings.

Just before serving, add wine. Garnish with lemon slices and chives.

VARIATION Add 1/2 cup finely chopped cooked spinach or Swiss chard and top with sliced hard-cooked eggs.

NOTE If using canned consommé, dilute first and reduce salt called for in recipe.

LENTIL AND SPLIT PEA PUREE

Serves 6

2 slices bacon, diced
Rendered beef or chicken fat
  and/or butter as needed
1/2 cup minced onion and/or
  white of leek
1 large garlic clove, minced
1 carrot, thinly sliced
1/2 cup *each* dried brown
  lentils and yellow split peas
3 cups *each* dark beef and
  brown chicken stock
Salt and black pepper to taste
Dry red wine to taste
  (optional)
Minced green onion tops or
  tender celery leaves

Cook bacon until crisp, remove with slotted spoon to
drain on paper toweling and
set aside. Adding fat to bacon
drippings if needed, lightly
brown onion, garlic and carrot.
Stir in lentils and peas to coat
well and add stocks. Cover,
bring to gentle boil, lower
heat and simmer 40 minutes
or until legumes are soft.

Purée and reheat. Season with
salt and pepper and add wine.
Garnish with onion tops.

VARIATION Add with stock 1
or 2 ripe tomatoes, peeled
and chopped.

WHITE BEAN SOUP

Serves 6 to 8

1 cup minced onions
1 cup chopped celery with
  some leaves
1/2 cup minced leeks (white
  and some green)
3 tablespoons butter
2 cups dried Great Northern
  beans
6 cups chicken stock
1 small ham hock, blanched
  and rinsed
1 calf's tongue, blanched and
  rinsed
Bouquet garni of
  3 sprigs parsley
  1 sprig thyme
  1 bay leaf
  6 black peppercorns, lightly
    crushed
1/2 teaspoon salt
1/4 teaspoon white pepper
Dash cayenne pepper
2 tablespoons butter, cut into
  bits
1/2 cup minced fresh parsley
Paprika
Prepared horseradish
Rye bread

Sauté onions, celery and leeks
in 3 tablespoons butter until
onions are soft. Combine with
beans, stock, ham hock, tongue,
bouquet garni, salt, pepper
and cayenne. Cover, bring to
boil, lower heat and simmer 2
hours.

Discard bouquet garni. Remove ham hock and tongue
and cut as much into dice as
desired. Return diced meat to
soup, heat and adjust seasonings to taste.

Stir in butter and parsley
and sprinkle with paprika.
Pass horseradish and rye bread.

VARIATION Add 1 cup tomato
juice and sliced cooked Polish
sausages. Reheat.

DRIED LIMA BEAN AND CORN SOUP

Serves 4 to 6

1/2 cup dried baby lima beans
1 small onion, halved
1 whole small garlic clove,
    lightly mashed
2 cups water, boiling
2/3 cup coarsely cracked
    dried corn
1/4 cup minced onion
1 large garlic clove, minced
2 tablespoons rendered
    chicken fat and/or butter
4 cups brown chicken stock
Salt and black pepper to taste
1 large ripe tomato, peeled
    and diced
Minced fresh parsley and/or
    chives

Combine beans, onion and whole garlic clove in saucepan and pour boiling water over. Cover, bring to gentle boil and boil 2 minutes. Turn off heat and let stand 1 hour.

Lightly brown corn, minced onion and minced garlic in chicken fat. Add stock and beans and their liquid. Cover, bring to gentle boil, lower heat and simmer 30 minutes or until beans are softened but still retain their shape. Season with salt and pepper and stir in tomato. Garnish generously with parsley.

PINTO BEAN SOUP

Serves 6 to 8

1 cup chopped onion
1/2 cup chopped celery
1/4 cup *each* chopped carrot
    and leek (white and some
    green)
1 garlic clove, minced
3 tablespoons olive oil
1-1/4 cups dried pinto beans
1 ham hock, blanched and
    rinsed
6 cups pork stock
3 cups peeled and chopped
    ripe tomatoes
Bouquet garni of
    2 whole cloves
    1 bay leaf
    6 black peppercorns,
        lightly crushed
    4 sprigs parsley
1/4 teaspoon salt
1/4 teaspoon black pepper
1 cup tomato sauce
Minced fresh coriander

Sauté onion, celery, leek, carrot and garlic in oil until onion is soft. Add beans, ham hock, stock, tomatoes, bouquet garni, salt and pepper. Cover, bring to boil and simmer 2-1/2 to 3 hours. Discard bouquet garni.

Remove ham hock, cut meat into strips and reserve. Purée 2 cups of soup (with some beans) and return to rest of soup.

Add ham strips and tomato sauce, reheat and adjust seasonings. Sprinkle with coriander.

VARIATION Add 1 cup cooked pasta.

GARBANZO BEAN SOUP

Serves 6 to 8
1 cup minced onions
1/2 cup minced leeks (white
   and some green)
1/4 cup minced bell pepper
2 teaspoons minced garlic
1/4 cup olive oil
2 cups dried garbanzo beans,
   soaked
4 cups beef or lamb stock
1 small ham hock
1 teaspoon paprika
1/2 teaspoon salt
1/4 teaspoon black pepper
Pinch saffron threads
2 garlic sausages, sliced and
   sautéed in 1/2 tablespoon
   butter
Garlic croutons

Sauté onions, leeks, bell pepper and garlic in oil until
onion is soft. Add garbanzo
beans and their liquid, stock,
ham hock and seasonings.
Cover, bring to boil, lower
heat and simmer until garbanzo beans are tender, adding
water or stock if needed.

Remove ham hock and cut meat into small dice. Return diced ham to soup and adjust seasonings to taste. Add sausage slices and serve with garlic croutons.

VARIATION Add diced potatoes the last 15 minutes of cooking and garnish with minced fresh mint.

CREAMY WHITE BEAN SOUP

Serves 6
3/4 cup dried small white
   beans
1-1/2 cups water
1/2 teaspoon salt
1-1/2 cups thinly sliced onions
1/2 cup *each* chopped celery
   and celery leaves
1/2 cup chopped carrot
1/2 cup minced fresh parsley
2 tablespoons *each* olive oil
   and butter
5 cups veal and/or chicken
   stock
1/2 cup tomato sauce
1 teaspoon minced fresh basil
1/4 teaspoon white pepper
1 cup half-and-half cream
Chiffonade of sorrel and
   spinach (page 172)

Cook beans in water and salt 1 hour, adding more water if needed.

Cook vegetables and parsley in oil and butter, covered, 30 minutes. Do not brown.

Add stock, tomato sauce, basil, pepper and beans with their liquid. Cover, bring to boil, lower heat and simmer 1 hour or until beans are tender.

Purée, reheat with cream and adjust seasonings to taste.

Serve with a portion of chiffonade in each bowl.

VARIATION Ladle soup into 6 ovenproof bowls; sprinkle each with 2 tablespoons grated sharp Cheddar cheese and broil to melt cheese.

CUBAN BLACK BEAN SOUP

A highly seasoned soup that can be served as a main meal with rice.

Serves 8 to 10
1 pound dried Latin American
   black beans*, soaked
10 cups water

2 teaspoons salt
1 cup *each* minced onion and
   bell pepper
3/4 cup minced celery and
   leaves
3/4 cup minced carrots
6 tablespoons olive oil
5 garlic cloves, minced
1 teaspoon ground cumin, or
   to taste
1 tablespoon white vinegar
1 teaspoon Maggi's seasoning
Salt and black pepper to taste
Minced onions
Sieved hard-cooked egg yolk
*See glossary

Cook beans in water and salt until soft. While beans are cooking, sauté onion, bell pepper, celery and carrots in oil until onions are brown. Add garlic, cumin, vinegar and Maggi's seasoning. Cook, stirring, 3 minutes.

Drain a little water from the beans, add to vegetables, and cook slowly, covered, 30 minutes. Combine with beans, adding more water if needed. Reheat and adjust seasonings with salt and pepper. Pass bowls of minced onions (soaked in olive oil and vinegar, if desired) and sieved egg yolk.

Grain Soups

MILLET-VEGETABLE SOUP

Cultivated from ancient times, millet is a very nutritious grain. Today it is a popular staple in India and in Middle Eastern and African countries.

Serves 4 to 6
2/3 cup millet
2 cups diced root vegetables, such as carrots, celery, onions, leeks, kohlrabi, turnips, parsnips, celery root
1 cup sliced mushrooms (optional)
1 medium potato, scrubbed and diced
2 large garlic cloves, minced
4 tablespoons rendered chicken fat or butter
6 cups stock of choice
Salt and black pepper to taste
Minced fresh parsley and/or chives or green onion tops

Sauté millet, vegetables and garlic in rendered chicken fat until lightly browned. Add stock, cover, bring to gentle boil, lower heat and simmer 30 minutes until millet is tender. Season with salt and pepper and garnish with parsley.

VARIATION Add cooked vegetables, such as peas, corn, sliced beans, broccoli flowerets.

CAULIFLOWER-BROWN RICE SOUP

Serves 6
1/3 cup raw brown rice
1 medium onion, chopped
1 large leek, chopped (white and some green)
1/3 cup chopped bell pepper (optional)
2 tablespoons butter and/or rendered chicken fat
6 cups brown chicken stock
3 large ripe tomatoes, peeled and chopped
1 medium head cauliflower, broken into flowerets
1/2 teaspoon ground mace
Salt and white pepper to taste
Minced fresh parsley
Garlic croutons

Brown the rice, onion, leek and bell pepper in butter until golden. Add 2 cups of the stock and the tomatoes. Cover and cook gently 30 minutes. Add all but 1/2 cup of the cauliflowerets and seasonings. Cover and cook 10 minutes or until rice is tender. Purée and return to saucepan. Add remaining stock, reheat, adjust seasonings and garnish with reserved cauliflowerets, parsley and croutons.

STEEL-CUT OATS AND BEET SOUP

Serves 3
1/2 cup steel-cut oats
1/4 cup *each* minced onion and celery
2 tablespoons rendered chicken fat and/or butter
3 cups brown chicken stock
2 medium beets, cooked and cut in julienne
Salt and black pepper to taste
Minced fresh parsley and/or chives

Brown oats, onion and celery in chicken fat. Add stock, bring to gentle boil, cover, lower heat and simmer 20 minutes, or until oats are tender but still crunchy. Add beets, reheat and season with salt and pepper. Garnish with parsley.

BULGHUR SOUP WITH BEET GREENS

Serves 3 or 4
3/4 cup *fine* bulghur
2 tablespoons rendered beef or chicken fat and/or butter
4 cups dark beef stock or brown chicken stock
3 cups finely shredded tender young beet greens
Salt and black pepper to taste

Brown bulghur in beef fat, add stock, cover, bring to gentle boil, lower heat and simmer 15 minutes or until bulghur is tender. Raise heat, add beet greens, cover and cook 3 minutes over medium heat until greens are tender. Season with salt and pepper.

FOUR-GRAIN VEGETABLE SOUP

Serves 8 to 10
1 large carrot, sliced
1 large rib celery, sliced
1 turnip, diced
1 large leek, sliced (white and some green)
1 onion, diced
4 tablespoons rendered chicken fat or butter, or as needed
1/2 cup *each* millet, brown rice, hulled barley and wheat berries
8 to 10 cups stock of choice
2 to 3 cups peeled and chopped ripe tomatoes
1/2 cup minced fresh parsley
2 large bay leaves
Salt and black pepper to taste
2 to 3 cups shredded Swiss chard, spinach, kale or other greens
Freshly grated Parmesan cheese

Brown carrot, celery, turnip, leek and onion in rendered chicken fat. Remove with slotted spoon and set aside. Adding more fat if needed, brown grains, stirring constantly. Add 4 cups of the stock, tomatoes, parsley and bay leaves. Cover, bring to boil, lower heat and simmer 30 minutes. Add reserved browned vegetables, bring back to simmer and cook 15 minutes until grains and vegetables are tender but still retain their identity. Discard bay leaves, add remaining stock, reheat and add salt and pepper to taste. Bring to boil and stir in chard. Cook just until tender. Serve with Parmesan cheese.

Worried about too much salt in your diet? Try one of the many vegetable salts or salt substitutes available in health-food and natural-food stores and some markets. Fresh lemon juice also adds a salty flavor.

Romanic Soups

Of soup and love the first is the best.
—*Spanish Proverb*

Perhaps the Roman Empire left more than its language as a heritage to France, Spain, Italy and Portugal. These Mediterranean countries are all unsurpassed in the culinary arts, especially in imaginative soup making.

French Soups

SOUPE A L'OIGNON GRATINEE
French Onion Soup

Serves 6
4 cups thinly sliced onions (1 pound)
1 teaspoon sugar
4 tablespoons butter and/or rendered chicken fat
1 tablespoon olive oil
2 garlic cloves, finely minced
2 tablespoons unbleached flour
1/4 teaspoon dry mustard
1/4 cup cognac, heated
2 cups *each* dark beef and brown chicken stock
1-1/4 cups Beef Consommé (page 20)
1/4 teaspoon freshly grated nutmeg
1/8 teaspoon black pepper
1/2 teaspoon Worcestershire sauce
Salt to taste
1/2 cup dry vermouth or dry white wine
6 rusks or sourdough French bread slices, toasted
6 tablespoons *each* freshly grated Gruyère and Parmesan, or Comté or Beaufort, or crumbled Gorgonzola cheese

Slowly brown onions and sugar in butter and oil. Add garlic, cook 3 minutes and sprinkle with flour and mustard. Cook, stirring, 3 minutes, raise heat and pour cognac over. Ignite and let burn down. Add stocks, consommé, nutmeg, pepper and Worcestershire sauce. Cover, bring to boil, lower heat and simmer 20 minutes. Add salt, if needed.

Cool and refrigerate overnight to mellow the flavor. Reheat and adjust seasonings to taste. Just before serving add vermouth.

Ladle soup into ovenproof bowls, top with rusks or toast sprinkled with cheese and broil to melt cheese.

VARIATION Substitute red wine for the vermouth. Sprinkle with minced fresh parsley and paprika.

SOUPE DE COMPIEGNE
Creamy Onion Soup

Serves 4
1-1/2 cups diced onions
1/8 teaspoon sugar
4 tablespoons butter
1/2 teaspoon dry mustard
3 cups lamb stock
1 cup milk
1 egg yolk, beaten
1/2 cup heavy cream
Salt and cayenne pepper
  to taste
Slivered pimiento
Minced fresh parsley and/or
  chives

Sauté onions sprinkled with sugar in butter until starting to turn golden. Sprinkle with mustard and cook 2 minutes. Add stock, cover, bring to boil, lower heat and simmer until onions are soft.

Purée, add milk and heat. Beat egg yolk and cream, whisk in 1/2 cup of hot soup, return to rest of soup and reheat. Do not boil.

Adjust seasonings to taste with salt and cayenne and serve with a garnish of slivered pimiento and parsley.

VARIATION Add a chiffonade (page 172) of chicory and sprinkle with paprika.

POTAGE FINES HERBES
Herb Soup

Serves 4
1 cup chopped sorrel
1/2 cup *each* chopped lettuce,
  chervil and watercress
3/4 cup chopped leeks (white
  only)
2 garlic cloves, minced
2 teaspoons minced fresh dill
1 tablespoon butter
1/2 tablespoon unbleached
  flour
2 cups brown chicken stock
1 teaspoon minced fresh
  savory
1/2 teaspoon minced fresh
  basil
1 cup diced potato
1-1/2 cups half-and-half
  cream or milk
2 egg yolks, beaten
1/2 cup heavy cream
Salt and white pepper to taste
Watercress sprigs

Sauté herbs and vegetables in butter 5 minutes, stirring to coat well.

Sprinkle with flour, cook, stirring, 3 minutes and gradually add stock. Cook and stir until smooth. Add savory, basil and potato. Cover, bring to boil and cook until potatoes are soft. Purée.

Reheat with half-and-half cream. Beat together yolks and heavy cream, whisk in 1/2 cup hot soup and return to rest of soup. Heat, but do not boil. Adjust seasonings with salt and pepper. Serve with sprigs of watercress.

Try growing your own watercress or curlycress in a shady spot with lots of water. They reseed themselves and the young plants make excellent garnishes.

POTAGE PUREE D'AUBERGINES
Eggplant Purée

Serves 4 to 6

1 medium eggplant, diced
   (2-1/2 to 3 cups)
1/4 cup minced mushrooms
2 tablespoons minced green
   onions and tops
1 garlic clove, minced
2 tablespoons olive oil
4 cups lamb stock
Pinch sugar
1-1/2 teaspoons tomato paste
1/4 cup dry red wine
1 tablespoon butter
1 tablespoon unbleached flour
1/4 teaspoon crumbled dried
   sage
3/4 cup heavy cream
Salt and white pepper to taste
Diced tomato
Plain yoghurt

Cook eggplant, mushrooms, onions and garlic in oil, covered, 10 minutes. Stir frequently.

Add stock, sugar, tomato paste and wine. Cover, bring to boil, lower heat and simmer until eggplant is soft. Force through sieve and push as much pulp through as possible, leaving the skin.

Melt butter until bubbly, sprinkle with flour and sage and cook, stirring, 3 minutes. Gradually add eggplant purée; cook and stir until smooth and slightly thickened.

Add cream, reheat without boiling and adjust seasonings to taste with more sage, salt and pepper. Garnish with diced tomato and pass a bowl of yoghurt.

POTAGE DUBARRY
Cauliflower Soup

Serves 6

4 cups cauliflowerets
1 cup *each* chopped celery
   and onion
1/4 cup chopped carrot
3 tablespoons butter and/or
   rendered chicken fat
3 tablespoons rice flour
1 teaspoon curry powder
4 cups chicken or veal stock
1/8 teaspoon white pepper
Dash cayenne pepper
1 cup *each* milk and half-
   and-half cream
2 teaspoons fresh lemon juice
Salt
Minced fresh parsley

Reserve 1/2 cup tiny flowerets for garnish. Sauté remainder with celery, onion and carrot in butter until well coated and softened.

Sprinkle with flour and curry powder, cook, stirring, 3 minutes and gradually add stock. Cook and stir until smooth and slightly thickened.

Season with peppers, and cover and simmer 30 minutes. Purée, add milk and cream, and heat.

Add lemon juice and salt and adjust to taste. Garnish with reserved raw cauliflowerets and parsley.

POTAGE GERMINY
Sorrel Soup

Serves 6
4 cups chopped sorrel
2 tablespoons butter
2 tablespoons rendered
  chicken fat
1 tablespoon unbleached flour
4 cups chicken broth
1/8 teaspoon white pepper
3 egg yolks, beaten
2 cups half-and-half cream
Salt
Fresh lemon juice, dry sherry
  or Madeira
Paprika
Minced fresh parsley
Lemon toast fingers

Sauté sorrel in butter and chicken fat until limp and discolored. Sprinkle with flour, cook, stirring, 3 minutes and gradually add stock. Cook and stir until smooth and slightly thickened. Season with pepper, cover, bring to boil, lower heat and simmer 15 to 20 minutes, stirring occasionally. Purée.

Beat together egg yolks and cream, whisk in 1/2 cup hot soup and return to rest of soup. Reheat without boiling.

Adjust seasonings to taste with salt and lemon juice. Sprinkle with paprika and parsley and serve with lemon toast fingers.

VARIATION Basil, marjoram and lovage complement sorrel; if you have an herb garden use them.

POTAGE SAINT-CLOUD
Fresh Pea Soup

Serves 6
6 cups shelled green peas
6 cups chicken stock
Bouquet garni of
  1/2 onion
  1 garlic clove
  1 sprig thyme
  1 sprig chervil
  4 sprigs parsley
  3 basil leaves
  2 green onions and tops,
    cut up
  1 bay leaf
1 teaspoon ground turmeric
1 cup heavy cream
1/2 teaspoon salt
1/8 teaspoon white pepper
Dry sherry to taste
Minced fresh chervil or
  parsley
Croutons

Combine peas, stock, bouquet garni and turmeric; cover, bring to boil and cook 5 minutes or until peas are just tender-crisp. Remove 1/2 cup of peas and reserve. Continue cooking remaining peas 30 minutes. Purée.

Reheat with cream and season with salt and pepper. Adjust seasonings to taste. Add reserved peas and sherry. Garnish with chervil and pass croutons.

VARIATION Substitute lamb stock for chicken stock. Add 1 cup cooked white rice to purée. Reheat, adjust seasonings and add a chiffonade of sorrel (page 172).

If frozen peas must be substituted for fresh, defrost and then, unless puréeing, just barely cook.

POTAGE PUREE
LAITUES ET POIS
Lettuce and Pea Purée

Serves 4

3 cups shredded romaine or
  red-leaf lettuce
3 cups shelled green peas
2 tablespoons butter and/or
  rendered chicken fat
1 teaspoon curry powder or
  to taste
4 cups chicken stock
Salt and white pepper to taste
Half-and-half cream (optional)
Minced fresh parsley and/or
  chives

Sauté lettuce and peas in butter until lettuce is wilted. Sprinkle with curry powder and cook, stirring, 3 minutes. Add stock and seasonings, cover, bring to gentle boil, lower heat and simmer 20 minutes. Purée, reheat with cream, if desired, adjust seasonings and garnish with parsley.

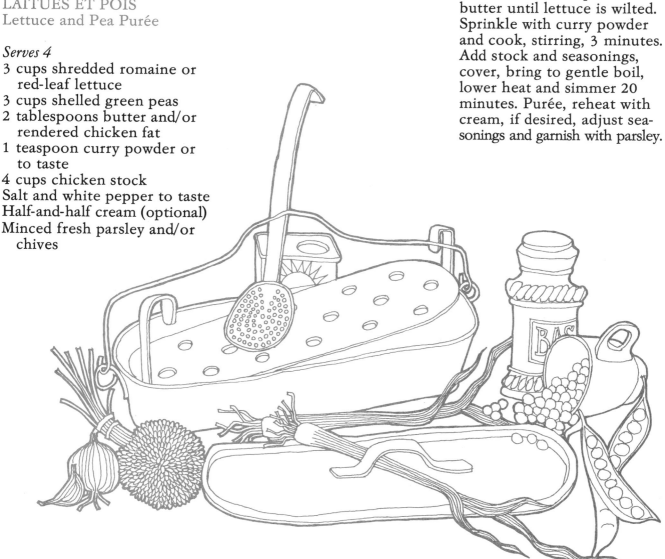

SOUPE DE LAITUES
Lettuce Soup

Serves 6

3 cups shredded iceberg or
 romaine lettuce
4 cups dark beef stock
1 cup chopped watercress
1/4 cup minced onion
2 tablespoons minced bell
 pepper
1 garlic clove, minced
1 teaspoon minced fresh
 tarragon
2 tablespoons minced fresh
 parsley
3 tablespoons butter
1/8 teaspoon freshly grated
 nutmeg
1/8 teaspoon white pepper
2 tablespoons raw brown or
 white rice
1 cup half-and-half cream or
 milk
2 egg yolks, beaten
3/4 cup heavy cream
Salt and black pepper to taste
Herb croutons

In blender or food processor, finely chop lettuce, a cup or so at a time, using stock if needed for moisture. Add to rest of stock with watercress.

Sauté onion, bell pepper, garlic and herbs in butter until soft; add seasonings and combine with stock mixture. Add rice. Cover, bring to boil, lower heat and simmer gently 30 minutes.

Add half-and-half cream and heat. Beat together yolks and heavy cream, whisk in 1/2 cup hot soup and return to rest of soup. Reheat; do not boil. Adjust seasonings with salt and pepper.

Serve with generous portions of croutons.

VARIATION Add cooked peas, chopped water chestnuts and minced green onions. Sprinkle with a bit of shredded raw lettuce.

POTAGE VELOUTE DE CHAMPIGNONS
Creamy Mushroom Soup

Serves 6

1 pound mushrooms
1 tablespoon butter
1/2 cup minced onion
1/4 cup minced celery
1 garlic clove, minced
3 tablespoons butter and/or
 olive oil
1/8 teaspoon dry mustard
Pinch cayenne pepper
1/4 teaspoon freshly grated
 lemon peel
2 tablespoons unbleached
 flour
6 cups chicken or beef stock
1 teaspoon fresh lemon juice,
 or to taste
3 sprigs parsley
1 sprig thyme or 1/2 teaspoon
 dried thyme
2 egg yolks, beaten
3/4 cup heavy cream
2 tablespoons butter, softened
Salt
Paprika
Minced fresh chervil

Reserve 8 mushroom caps, slice and sauté them in 1 tablespoon butter. Slice the remaining mushrooms.

Sauté onion, celery and garlic in 3 tablespoons butter until soft; add uncooked mushrooms and seasonings and cook until slightly browned. Sprinkle with flour; cook, stirring, 3 minutes. Gradually add stock and lemon juice. Cook and stir until smooth and slightly thickened. Add parsley and thyme, cover and simmer 30 minutes. Strain.

Add reserved sautéed mushrooms and simmer 5 minutes; beat together yolks and cream, whisk in 1/2 cup hot soup and return to rest of soup. Reheat, but do not boil. Swirl in butter, adjust seasonings with salt and serve with sprinkling of paprika and chervil.

VARIATION Omit the liaison of yolks and cream and add 1/3 cup dry sherry and 1/2 cup half-and-half cream. Pour into ovenproof bowls, spread with salted whipped cream and slivered almonds, and broil briefly to brown cream.

POTAGE PAYSANNE
Peasant Soup

Serves 6

5 cups brown chicken stock
1 tablespoon beef stock base
1/2 cup minced leek (white and some green)
1 carrot, chopped
1 turnip, chopped
1 potato, diced
1-1/2 cups shelled green peas
4 cabbage leaves
6 lettuce leaves
6 sprigs *each* parsley and watercress
6 to 8 large fresh mint leaves
1 tablespoon minced fresh dill
1 cup half-and-half cream
2 tablespoons fresh lemon juice
2 tablespoons butter
1/4 teaspoon black pepper
1/2 teaspoon salt
Sour cream

Simmer stock, stock base, vegetables, parsley and watercress until vegetables are soft. Add mint and dill; purée.

Reheat with cream, lemon juice and butter. Season with pepper and salt and adjust to taste.

Serve with dollops of sour cream.

VARIATIONS Garnish with chopped watercress and diced tomato. For a heartier soup, add sliced cooked sausage. Dry vermouth adds a special zest.

When thickening with egg yolk and cream liaison, always wait until the last minute. Reheating or keeping warm may curdle the soup.

Spanish Soups

According to Catalonians Jorge Rosell and his wife, gazpacho is served with green tomatoes and is more a salad than a soup. They offer the following six soup ideas as truly representative of Catalonia, Spain, where garlic, onion, and pimentón, in descending order, are the most popular seasonings.

SOPA DE CALABEZA
Pumpkin Soup

Serves 6

6 cups chicken or beef stock
2 pounds fresh pumpkin*, peeled and cubed
4 garlic cloves, minced
1-1/2 cups minced onions
1/4 to 1/2 cup minced fresh coriander
Salt and black pepper to taste
Bread cubes fried in garlic olive oil
Coriander sprigs

Combine stock, pumpkin, garlic cloves, onion, and minced coriander and cook until pumpkin is tender. Purée, reheat and adjust seasonings with salt and pepper.

Serve hot with fried bread cubes and garnish with coriander sprigs.

*Imported from Puerto Rico almost year round. Lighter, more delicate in flavor than those from the States.

NOTE The flavor of coriander grows stronger if soup is made ahead and reheated. Can be served cold if nongelatinous stock is used.

SOPA DE JUDIAS BLANCOS
White Bean Soup

Serves 4 to 6
4 garlic cloves
1 onion, quartered
1 ham hock
1 cup dried Great Northern beans, rinsed and drained
6 cups water
1/2 teaspoon salt
1 wedge cabbage (1/8 head)
1 carrot, halved
1 small rib celery, halved
Garlic croutons

Tie garlic, onion and ham hock in cheesecloth for easy removal. Combine with beans, water and salt. Cover, bring to boil, lower heat and simmer 1-1/2 hours, or until beans are almost tender.

Tie cabbage, carrot and celery in cheesecloth and add to soup. Continue cooking until vegetables are tender, adding water as needed.

Remove vegetables and ham hock and place on platter to be served with the soup. Ladle soup into bowls and serve with garlic croutons.

VARIATION Add peeled and chopped ripe tomatoes after removing ham hock. Reheat.

Fresh coriander has aliases—Chinese parsley, cilantro.

SOPA DE AJO
Garlic Soup

Serves 6
6 cups water
1 teaspoon salt
20 whole garlic cloves
2 teaspoons olive oil
4 eggs, beaten
6 stale French bread slices
Freshly ground black pepper

Bring water, salt and garlic to boil, lower heat and simmer 30 minutes. Remove garlic and add olive oil. Bring back to boil and gradually add eggs; let cook gently until eggs are set.

Add bread slices and let them soak up the broth. Serve immediately and pass the peppermill.

VARIATION For true garlic lovers, press 5 of the garlic cloves removed from the soup and add them just before adding the bread slices.

SOPA DE ALMENDRAS
Almond Soup

Serves 4 to 6
1 tablespoon olive oil
1 tablespoon unbleached
  flour
2 cups chicken or veal stock
1 cup whole blanched
  almonds, ground
1/8 teaspoon *each* ground allspice and freshly grated
  nutmeg
1/4 teaspoon ground thyme
1/4 teaspoon salt
2 cups milk
1/4 cup slivered blanched
  almonds, dusted with 1/2
  teaspoon pimentón*
*See glossary

Heat oil, add flour and cook,
stirring, 3 minutes. Gradually
add stock; cook and stir until
smooth and slightly thickened.
Add ground almonds and seasonings; cover, bring to boil,
lower heat and simmer gently
30 minutes.
  Strain, forcing as much pulp
through sieve as possible. Add
milk, heat and adjust seasonings to taste. Garnish with
slivered almonds that have
been dusted with pimentón.

NOTE Good before a lamb
dinner. Or serve as a luncheon
soup with fruit salad and
chicken sandwiches.

ESCUDELLA
Bean Soup

A garlicky main-meal soup!

Serves 6 to 8
1/2 cup dried garbanzo beans,
  soaked in water to cover
  8 hours
1/2 cup dried small white
  beans (navy or pea)
6 cups water, or as needed
One 8-ounce ham hock,
  blanched and rinsed
One 4-ounce piece lean pork
One 8-ounce lean short rib
1 whole small cabbage
9 garlic cloves, pressed
1 onion, cut into eighths
6 to 8 small whole potatoes
12 to 16 Pilotas (following)
Salt
French bread
Freshly ground black pepper

Combine garbanzo beans,
white beans, water, ham hock,
pork and short rib. Cover,
bring to boil, lower heat and
simmer 1-1/4 hours, or until
beans start to soften; add

water if needed.
  Make 1/2-inch-deep slits in
a spoke pattern on core of
cabbage. Add with garlic,
onion and potatoes; cook at
medium boil 5 minutes. Add
Pilotas and cook 10 minutes.
  Adjust seasonings with salt,
adding boiling water if needed
to make 6 to 8 cups liquid.
  Remove cabbage and meat
and place on platter to be
served with the soup.
  Place 1 potato and 2 Pilotas
in each bowl and ladle soup
over. Serve with French bread
and pass the peppermill.

PILOTAS

Makes 12 to 16
1/4 pound *each* ground lean
  beef and pork
1/2 teaspoon unbleached flour
1 garlic clove, pressed
1 tablespoon finely minced
  fresh parsley
1 teaspoon salt
1 egg white, beaten

Combine meat, flour, garlic,
parsley and salt. With floured
hands, roll into 12 or 16
football-shaped balls. Roll
each ball in flour and then
beaten egg white.

GAZPACHO

Serves 4 to 6

2 cups French bread cubes,
  soaked in 3 cups water
4 teaspoons minced garlic
1/2 cup minced onion
4 tomatoes, peeled and diced
3 tablespoons *each* olive oil
  and cider vinegar

1/2 teaspoon salt
1/4 teaspoon black pepper
6 drops Tabasco sauce
1/8 teaspoon ground cumin
Diced green tomato
Coriander sprigs
Freshly ground black pepper

Purée ingredients, except diced tomato and coriander sprigs, and chill.

Adjust seasonings and serve in chilled bowls; garnish with a generous amount of green tomato and sprigs of coriander. Pass the peppermill.

SOPA DE GALLINA
Chicken Soup

Serves 6

6 cups brown chicken stock, made with extra onion, fresh coriander and lots of garlic
1 cup cooked fideos (small pasta shells), rice or diced potatoes
Pinch saffron threads, or to taste
Salt
Freshly ground black pepper

Heat stock and fideos. Stir in saffron and adjust seasonings with salt. Pass the peppermill.

VARIATION For a heartier meal, add shredded tops of Chinese turnips (closest to vegetable available in Spain) and hunto to taste. (Hunto, a type of pork fat aged 6 or more months, adds an unusual flavor. Sometimes available in Mexican markets.)

SOPA DE ARROZ
Rice Soup

Serves 3 or 4

3 cups water or stock
1/2 teaspoon salt
2 to 4 garlic cloves, pressed
1/2 cup raw white rice, well washed
2 teaspoons olive oil

Bring water, salt and garlic to boil. Add rice, cover, bring back to boil, lower heat and simmer 15 minutes, or until rice is tender. Drizzle oil over, cover and remove from heat. Let stand 5 minutes without stirring before serving.

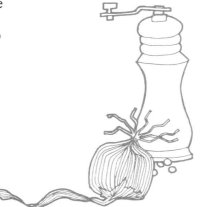

Italian Soups

MINESTRONE

This Italian classic of vegetables with pasta can be almost anything you wish to make it. With Italian or French bread and a light salad, it often makes a full meal, though it needn't be that hearty. Some say never use smoked ham or bacon; others maintain such flavors are essential. A prosciutto bone is considered a must by still others. The two recipes that follow are flexible and interchangeable. Use whatever is at hand.

MINESTRONE WITH BASIL

Serves 8 to 10

2 slices bacon, diced
2 cups chopped onions
1/2 pound Italian sausage, chopped, browned and drained

8 cups beef stock
2 tablespoons minced fresh
  basil
1/2 cup minced fresh Italian
  parsley
1 garlic clove, pressed
1/4 teaspoon black pepper
Pinch cayenne pepper
1/2 teaspoon salt
3 cups diced potatoes
1/2 cup soup pasta
4 cups loosely packed torn
  spinach or Swiss chard
  leaves
Croutons
Freshly grated Parmesan or
  Romano cheese

Sauté bacon and onions until
golden. Add sausage, stock,
basil, parsley, garlic, peppers,
salt and potatoes. Cover, bring
to boil and cook 10 minutes.

Add soup pasta and cook 6
minutes. Add spinach, bring
back to boil to just cook the
spinach. Adjust seasonings to
taste.

Serve with croutons and
Parmesan cheese.

MINESTRONE WITH NAVY BEANS

Serves 6 to 8

1/3 cup dried Great Northern or cranberry beans
1 ham hock, blanched and
  rinsed
1 garlic clove
1 small white onion
2 cups water
1/4 cup minced onion
1/2 cup minced leeks (white
  and some green)
1 garlic clove, minced
2 tablespoons olive oil
1/4 cup minced fresh herbs
  (Italian parsley, basil,
  savory, rosemary, oregano,
  thyme and/or sage)
6 cups chicken, beef or veal
  stock
2 cups sliced vegetables
  (carrots, turnips, parsnips,
  green or wax beans,
  asparagus, peas, escarole,
  potatoes)
1/2 cup soup pasta
1 tablespoon tomato paste
1/2 teaspoon salt
1/4 teaspoon black pepper
3/4 teaspoon dry mustard
Crumbled blue or Gorgonzola
  cheese

Combine beans, ham hock,
garlic clove, whole onion and
water. Cover, bring to boil,
lower heat and simmer 1-1/2
to 2 hours, or until meat is
tender, adding water as needed.
Remove ham hock and cut
meat into small pieces; set
meat aside. Discard garlic and
onion and set beans and their
liquid aside.

Sauté minced onion, leeks
and minced garlic in oil 5
minutes. Add herbs and cook
and stir a little longer to coat
well. Add stock, bring to boil
and add vegetables. Cook 5
to 10 minutes, depending on
which vegetables are used.
Keeping soup boiling, add
beans and their liquid, reserved
ham and pasta. Boil until
pasta is tender.

Add tomato paste, salt, pepper and dry mustard. Adjust
to taste and serve garnished
with crumbled blue cheese.

ZUPPA ALLA ESCAROLE
CON POLPETTI
Escarole Soup with Meatballs

Serves 6 to 8

1 pound marrow bones, sawed
  into 3-inch pieces
6 black peppercorns, lightly
  crushed
3 sprigs parsley
1 bay leaf
8 cups beef stock
1/2 teaspoon salt
2 tablespoons tomato paste
3/4 cup *each* diced onions,
  celery and carrots
1 cup diced potato
1 recipe Meatballs (following)
3/4 pound escarole or Austra-
  lian lettuce, shredded
Minced fresh Italian parsley
Freshly grated Parmesan
  cheese

Combine bones, peppercorns, parsley, bay leaf, stock, salt and tomato paste. Cover, bring to boil, lower heat and simmer 1 hour. Strain, cool, chill and defat.

Bring soup back to boil, add onion, celery and carrots and cook 10 minutes. Add potatoes and cook 5 more minutes.

Add meatballs and escarole and cook 10 minutes. Adjust seasonings.

Serve sprinkled with parsley. Pass Parmesan cheese.

MEATBALLS

3/4 pound ground round steak
1 egg
1 garlic clove, pressed
3 tablespoons minced fresh
    Italian parsley
1/2 teaspoon salt
1/4 teaspoon *each* black
    pepper and crumbled dried
    oregano
1/2 to 1 teaspoon fresh
    lemon juice
3 tablespoons freshly grated
    Romano or Parmesan cheese

Mix together all ingredients, chill, then form into walnut-sized balls.

ZUPPA ALLA VERMICELLI
Vermicelli Soup

Serves 8
1/2 pound vermicelli, broken
2 tablespoons *each* butter and
    olive oil
1/2 cup minced onion
1 garlic clove, minced
1 cup peeled, seeded and
    minced Italian tomatoes
8 cups dark beef or brown
    chicken stock
1/2 cup minced fresh Italian
    parsley
1/2 teaspoon salt
1/4 teaspoon black pepper
1 recipe Pilou (following)
Freshly grated Parmesan or
    Romano cheese

Take advantage of the new vegetable, soy and cornmeal pastas, in a variety of shapes, that are available in health-food stores.

Sauté vermicelli in butter and oil, stirring, until golden. Remove with slotted spoon and reserve. Add onion and garlic to pan and sauté until soft. Add tomatoes, stock, parsley and reserved vermicelli. Cover, bring to boil and cook until vermicelli is tender.

Adjust seasonings with salt and pepper. Mix Pilou in soup tureen and gradually pour soup over Pilou.

Pass Parmesan cheese.

VARIATIONS Add thinly sliced zucchini, cut green beans, corn kernels, green peas or other vegetables at the same time as the vermicelli.

PILOU

3 or 4 egg yolks
3 to 5 tablespoons olive oil

In soup tureen beat egg yolks until golden. Gradually add olive oil as if making mayonnaise, beating constantly until smooth but not as thick as mayonnaise.

ZUPPA MARITATA
Chicken Soup

Serves 6
1/4 cup minced green onions
    and tops
1/2 cup minced mushrooms
1 tablespoon olive oil
Dash cayenne pepper
1/4 teaspoon *each* salt and
    crumbled dried oregano
1 teaspoon fresh lemon juice
6 cups brown chicken stock,
    made with extra oregano
    and garlic
1/4 pound vermicelli, broken
1 recipe Chicken Balls (page
    171), cooked, or 1-1/2 cups
    diced cooked chicken
3 eggs, beaten
1 cup half-and-half cream
6 tablespoons freshly grated
    Romano cheese
Salt, black pepper and minced
    fresh oregano
Paprika
Minced fresh Italian parsley
Freshly grated Romano cheese

Sauté green onions and mushrooms in oil until soft, sprinkling with cayenne, salt, oregano and lemon juice while
cooking. Add stock, bring to
boil and stir in vermicelli.
Cook 7 minutes after the
soup comes back to a boil.
Reheat with Chicken Balls or
diced chicken.
  Beat together eggs and
cream, whisk in 1/2 cup of
hot soup and return to rest of
soup. Heat, but do not boil.
  Add Romano cheese and
adjust seasonings to taste with
salt, pepper and oregano.
  Sprinkle with paprika and
Italian parsley and pass extra
Romano cheese.

---

*Pasta should always be cooked
al dente.*

ZUPPA PAVESE
Consommé
with Toast and Eggs

Serves 4
5 cups Beef or Chicken
    Consommé (page 20)
Salt to taste
4 thick slices sourdough or
    Italian bread, fried in
    olive oil
4 small eggs
Paprika
Italian parsley sprigs

Bring consommé to boil. Season
with salt. Place a slice of
bread in each of 4 bowls,
carefully break an egg onto
each, and gradually pour hot
soup over the egg to cook it
slightly. (Poach the eggs first
if you prefer them cooked
solid.)
  Serve with a sprinkle of
paprika and Italian parsley
sprigs.

VARIATION Pass freshly grated
Parmesan or Romano cheese.

ZUPPA ALLA PISTOU
Soup with Basil

Serves 6 to 8

1 cup thinly sliced leeks
   (white only)
2 ribs celery, thinly sliced
   on diagonal
3/4 cup thinly sliced carrots
2 garlic cloves, minced
2 tablespoons olive oil
8 cups beef, chicken or
   veal broth
1-1/2 cups diced potatoes
1-1/2 cups diagonally cut
   green beans
1 bunch spinach, chopped
1-1/2 cups peeled and diced
   ripe tomatoes
1/2 teaspoon minced fresh
   thyme
1/4 teaspoon minced fresh
   rosemary
1/2 teaspoon black pepper
3/4 teaspoon paprika
1 teaspoon salt

1-1/2 cups shredded iceberg
   lettuce
1 recipe Pistou (following)
Freshly grated Parmesan
   cheese

Sauté leeks, celery, carrots
and garlic in oil until leeks
are soft; do not brown. Add
broth, bring to boil and add
potatoes. Cook 5 minutes.
Add beans, spinach, tomatoes
and seasonings, and bring back
to boil. Cook 10 minutes,
until potatoes are almost tender. Add lettuce and boil 3
minutes until tender-crisp.
Adjust seasonings.
   Whisk 1/2 cup of hot soup
into Pistou in tureen. Gradually beat in rest of soup.
Serve with Parmesan and extra
Pistou.

VARIATIONS For a heartier meal,
add cooked red or white beans,
pasta and additional vegetables, such as grated zucchini
and thinly sliced mushrooms,
with the lettuce.

PISTOU

1-1/2 teaspoons minced fresh
   basil
1 teaspoon minced garlic
1 ripe tomato, peeled, seeded
   and diced, or 1 teaspoon
   tomato paste
1/4 cup freshly grated Parmesan or Gruyère cheese
1/2 cup olive oil

Crush basil, garlic and tomato
in mortar and transfer to
soup tureen. Blend in cheese
and gradually add olive oil,
beating constantly. Remove
one-third to a small serving
bowl.

From the Americas

Worries go down better with soup than without.
—Yiddish Proverb

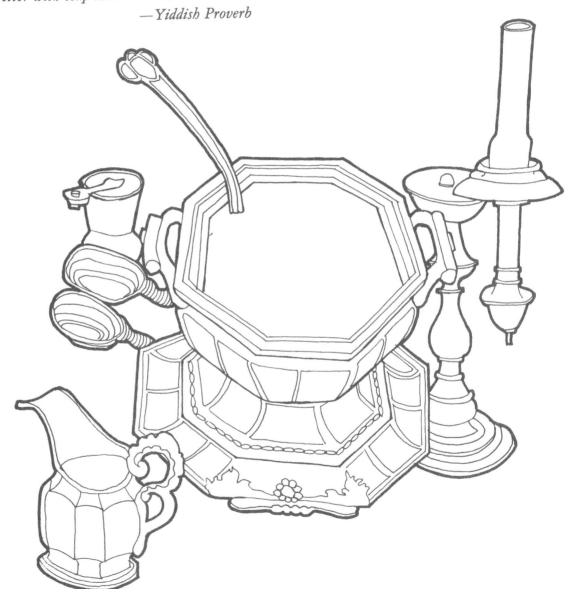

Traditional Old World soups abound in the New World, but the Americas have developed their own favorites, too. Chowders, for example, have gained world acclaim, and many interesting and delicious soups can be found in Central and South America.

ALBONDIGAS
Lamb Soup with Meatballs

Serves 6 to 8
6 cups lamb broth
3 cups peeled and chopped ripe tomatoes
1/4 cup minced bell pepper
1 rib celery and leaves, chopped
2 onions, sliced
6 whole cloves
1 bay leaf
1 tablespoon minced fresh dill
4 garlic cloves, minced
3 sprigs parsley
12 black peppercorns, lightly crushed
1/2 teaspoon salt
2 small zucchini, sliced
1/2 pound mushrooms, sliced
1 recipe Lamb Meatballs (following)
Dry sherry
Sour cream

Bring broth, tomatoes, vegetables, herbs and seasonings to boil, lower heat and simmer, covered, 2 hours. Strain. Bring stock mixture to boil, add zucchini and mushrooms; cook 10 minutes or until zucchini are tender-crisp.
  Adjust seasonings, add meatballs, and heat. Put 1 tablespoon dry sherry in each bowl and ladle in soup. Top with dollops of sour cream.

VARIATION Season with chili powder and ground cinnamon to taste, or sprinkle with freshly grated Parmesan or sharp Cheddar cheese.

LAMB MEATBALLS

1 pound lean lamb, ground
1/4 cup freshly grated Parmesan cheese
1 egg, beaten
1 tablespoon milk
1/4 cup minced fresh parsley
1/8 teaspoon minced fresh rosemary
1/2 teaspoon black pepper
1 tablespoon fresh lemon juice
1/4 cup fine bulghur (optional)

Mix together all ingredients, chill, form into balls the size of walnuts and brown on all sides. If bulghur is used, cover and cook 20 minutes.

No fresh herbs in your garden? Use one-third to one-half the amount dried.

MEXICAN CHILI SOUP

Serves 4
6 cups chicken stock
1/3 pound lean pork, diced
1/2 cup diced onion
1/2 cup raw fresh corn kernels
1 fresh jalapeno chili pepper,
    seeded and minced
1 cup sliced zucchini
1/2 cup tomato purée
Salt and black pepper to taste
Ripe avocado, cut into balls
    or cubes
Freshly grated Parmesan
    cheese

Combine all ingredients, except avocado and cheese, and simmer, covered, 30 minutes. Adjust seasonings to taste with salt and pepper. Just before serving add avocado balls. Pass grated Parmesan cheese.

CHUPE DE CAMARONES
Shrimp Soup

Serves 6
1 cup diced onion
2 garlic cloves, minced
2 ripe tomatoes, peeled and
    diced
1 to 2 teaspoons minced
    fresh chili pepper
1 tablespoon minced fresh
    oregano
1/4 cup olive oil
6 cups fish stock
1 teaspoon salt
1/2 teaspoon black pepper
1/2 cup raw white rice
3 medium potatoes, halved
1 cup raw fresh corn kernels
1-1/2 pounds medium shrimp,
    shelled and deveined
2 eggs, beaten with 1/4 cup
    freshly grated queso
    enchilado or imported
    Provolone
3/4 cup evaporated milk
Finely minced fresh parsley
    or coriander

Sauté onion, garlic, tomatoes, chili pepper and oregano in oil 5 minutes, stirring to blend. Add stock, salt and black pepper; bring to boil, add rice and potato halves, and cook, covered, 30 minutes, adding corn last 10 minutes.

Raise heat to boiling, add shrimp and cook 5 minutes. Do not overcook. Drizzle in egg and cheese mixture and boil 1 minute. Add milk, reheat and adjust seasonings to taste. Sprinkle with parsley and serve immediately.

CHUPE DE CARNE
Ground Beef Soup

Serves 6 to 8

1-1/2 cups minced onions

1/2 cup finely minced bell pepper

1 or 2 large garlic cloves, minced

2 tablespoons butter and/or corn oil

1-1/2 pounds ground lean beef

3/4 pound mushrooms, minced

1-1/2 teaspoons salt

1 teaspoon crumbled dried oregano

1/2 teaspoon *each* paprika and ground cumin

1/4 teaspoon black pepper

6 cups peeled and chopped ripe tomatoes

1 cup dried red kidney beans, cooked (page 52)

1-1/2 cups raw fresh corn kernels

1 recipe creamy mushroom concentrate (page 14)

1-1/2 cups freshly grated sharp Cheddar or Monterey Jack cheese

Freshly grated Parmesan cheese

Tortilla chips

Dried herbs and spices can sit on the shelf too long and lose much of their flavor. Especially true of ground cumin and chili and curry powders.

Sauté onions, bell pepper and garlic in butter until vegetables are soft. Raise heat, add meat and mushrooms, sprinkle with seasonings and herbs and cook and stir with fork until meat loses its color. Add rest of ingredients, except cheese and tortilla chips, mix well, cover, bring to gentle boil, lower heat and simmer 15 minutes. Add cheddar cheese and heat just until melted. Adjust seasonings and serve with Parmesan cheese and tortilla chips.

VARIATION Add any cooked vegetables, such as beans, peas, lima beans, or cooked macaroni shells, and reheat.

AVOCADO GAZPACHO

Serves 3 or 4

1 cup sour cream
1/2 cup milk
1 cup *each* tomato juice and
    tomato sauce
2 tablespoons fresh lemon
    juice
1 tablespoon olive oil
1 garlic clove, finely minced
1 bay leaf
1 cucumber, peeled, seeded
    and minced
1 tomato, peeled, seeded and
    diced
Salt, black pepper and
    Tabasco sauce to taste
2 avocados, mashed with
    1 tablespoon fresh lemon
    juice
Finely minced cucumber,
    peeled tomato and bell
    pepper
Garlic fingers

Beat sour cream well, then beat in milk, tomato juice, tomato sauce, lemon juice, oil and garlic. Combine well, add bay leaf, minced cucumber and diced tomato. Season with salt, pepper and Tabasco and chill thoroughly to blend flavors.

Remove bay leaf. Blend avocados into tomato mixture just before serving. Adjust seasonings and serve in chilled bowls. Garnish with finely minced cucumber, tomato and bell pepper, and serve with garlic fingers.

GARLIC SOUP

Serves 8

20 to 25 garlic cloves, peeled
1/4 cup olive oil
8 cups chicken stock
1 tablespoon chicken stock
    base
1/4 teaspoon *each* ground
    sage, ground thyme and
    black pepper
2 whole cloves
1/2 teaspoon *each* crumbled
    dried oregano and paprika
8 sprigs parsley
Salt
1/2 cup dry sherry
8 slices sourdough French
    bread, toasted
8 tablespoons *each* freshly
    grated Gruyère and
    Parmesan cheese

Sauté garlic in oil until just starting to turn golden. Add stock, stock base, seasonings and herbs. Cover, bring to boil, lower heat and simmer 1 hour.

Strain, reheat and adjust seasonings, adding salt if needed. Just before serving add sherry. Ladle soup into heated ovenproof bowls, top with toast, sprinkle with 1 tablespoon of each cheese, and broil to melt cheese.

VARIATION Omit cheese. Top each piece of toast with a small raw egg. Ladle hot soup over to poach egg and garnish with fresh minced coriander.

GARLIC SOUP WITH POTATO BALLS

Serves 6

6 medium potatoes, quartered
3/4 cup chopped onion
1 teaspoon salt
5 or more garlic cloves,
    pressed
2 egg yolks, beaten
1 cup olive oil
Salt and black pepper to taste
3 tablespoons unbleached
    flour
Minced fresh parsley or
    coriander

Combine potatoes, onion, 1/2 teaspoon of the salt and water to cover and boil until potatoes are soft. Drain, reserving liquid, and force potatoes through food mill or sieve.

Blend together garlic, remaining salt and egg yolks; gradually add oil, stirring constantly. Combine with sieved potato and reserve 3/4 cup. Add remaining garlic-potato mixture to reserved potato water and blend well. Adjust seasonings with salt and pepper.

Mix reserved potato-garlic mixture with flour, adding more flour if needed to form a mixture that can be shaped into balls. Form marble-sized balls, return soup to boil, add balls, lower heat slightly and cook 5 minutes. Garnish with parsley.

VARIATION Season with a little cider vinegar.

BLACK OLIVE SOUP

Serves 4

1-1/2 cups pitted ripe olives, sliced (reserve juice)
3 tablespoons grated onion
1/4 cup minced celery and leaves
2 garlic cloves
4 cups brown chicken stock
2 eggs, beaten
1 cup half-and-half cream
1 teaspoon Worcestershire sauce
1/2 teaspoon fresh lemon juice
1/4 cup juice from olives
Salt—be careful!
Tabasco sauce
Paprika
Grated onion

Simmer olives, onion, celery and garlic in stock, covered, for 20 minutes. Discard garlic.

Beat together eggs and cream, whisk in 1/2 cup hot stock, and return to rest of soup. Season with Worcestershire sauce and lemon juice. Add olive juice and adjust to taste with salt and Tabasco. Reheat and serve with a sprinkling of paprika and more grated onion.

VARIATION Cool, chill and serve in chilled bowls. Garnish with minced fresh parsley.

When thickening with egg yolk and cream liaison, always wait until the last minute. Reheating or keeping warm may curdle the soup.

CORN CHOWDER

Serves 6

4 or 5 ears corn
4 cups chicken stock
1 teaspoon sugar
1/2 teaspoon salt
1/2 cup minced onion
1/4 cup minced celery
4 tablespoons butter
1/2 teaspoon dry mustard
1/4 teaspoon black pepper
1 tablespoon fresh lemon juice
1-1/2 cups diced potatoes
2 cups half-and-half cream
3 drops Tabasco sauce
1/2 teaspoon Worcestershire sauce
1 egg yolk, beaten
3/4 cup heavy cream
3/4 teaspoon salt
1/4 teaspoon ground thyme
Paprika
Minced fresh parsley

Cut kernels from corn, scraping as much pulp and milk off as possible. Kernels should measure 2 cups. Boil cobs in stock with 1/2 teaspoon of the sugar and salt 15 minutes. Strain and reserve stock.

Sauté kernels, onion and celery in butter with mustard, remaining sugar and pepper until onions are soft but not browned. Add lemon juice, reserved stock and potatoes. Cover, bring to boil, lower heat and simmer 15 minutes. Add cream, Tabasco and Worcestershire sauce. Reheat. Beat together yolk and heavy cream, whisk in 1/2 cup hot soup and return to rest of soup. Heat, but do not boil. Season with salt and thyme and adjust to taste. Serve sprinkled with paprika and parsley.

CHEESE AND ONION SOUP

Serves 6
1-1/2 cups minced onion
4 tablespoons butter
3 tablespoons unbleached flour
1/2 teaspoon seasoned salt
Pinch cayenne pepper
1/4 teaspoon black pepper
1/2 teaspoon paprika
1/4 teaspoon ground sage
3 cups milk
1 cup half-and-half cream
2 cups freshly shredded sharp Cheddar cheese
1/2 teaspoon Worcestershire sauce
3 drops Tabasco sauce
3 tablespoons minced fresh parsley
Whipped cream
Minced fresh chives

Sauté onion in butter until soft. Add flour and seasonings, cook, stirring, 3 minutes and gradually add milk and cream. Cook and stir until smooth and thickened. Add cheese and stir until melted. Season with Worcestershire, Tabasco and parsley, and adjust to taste.

Garnish with dollops of whipped cream and sprinkle with chives.

Want to stretch your butter? To 1/4 pound softened butter, add 1 teaspoon liquid lecithin and 1 to 2 tablespoons safflower oil. Whirl in blender or processor.

CHEDDAR CHEESE VELOUTE

Serves 4 to 6
4 cups brown chicken stock
2 leeks, chopped (white only)
1/2 cup chopped onion
1/3 cup chopped celery
6 sprigs parsley
1/2 teaspoon ground turmeric
2 tablespoons cornstarch,
    mixed with 3 tablespoons
    cold water
1-1/2 cups freshly shredded
    sharp Cheddar cheese
1/4 teaspoon *each* white
    pepper, paprika, and
    freshly grated nutmeg
2 egg yolks, beaten
1-1/2 cups half-and-half
    cream or milk
1/3 cup dry white wine
Chili powder and salt to taste
Minced fresh chives
Paprika

Bring stock, vegetables, parsley and turmeric to boil, cover, lower heat and simmer 1 hour. Cool and strain.

Reheat, add cornstarch-water binder, and cook and stir until smooth and slightly thickened. Add cheese and seasonings and heat gently to melt cheese.

Beat together yolks and cream, whisk in 1/2 cup hot soup, and return to rest of soup. Reheat; do not boil. Add wine and adjust seasonings with chili powder and salt. Sprinkle with chives and paprika.

VARIATION Garnish with a generous amount of grated raw carrot.

CREAMY LOBSTER WITH CHEESE

Serves 3 or 4
One 8-ounce lobster tail,
    cooked and minced
1/4 cup dry sherry
3 tablespoons finely minced
    onion
1/2 teaspoon minced garlic
1 teaspoon finely minced
    shallots
2 tablespoons finely minced
    celery
2 tablespoons butter
1-1/2 tablespoons unbleached
    flour
2 cups half-and-half cream
2 tablespoons finely minced
    fresh parsley
1/4 teaspoon *each* salt and
    freshly grated lemon peel
1/8 teaspoon white pepper
1/4 cup freshly grated
    imported Provolone cheese
Paprika
Minced fresh chives

Soak lobster in sherry at least
1 hour. Cook onion, garlic,
shallots, and celery in butter,
covered, 10 minutes. Sprinkle
with flour, cook, stirring, 3
minutes and gradually add
cream. Cook and stir until
smooth and slightly thickened.
Add lobster and sherry and
parsley. Reheat and season
with salt, lemon peel and
pepper. Adjust to taste.

   Just before serving add
cheese and heat to melt. Thin
with milk, if desired. Dust
with paprika and sprinkle with
chives.

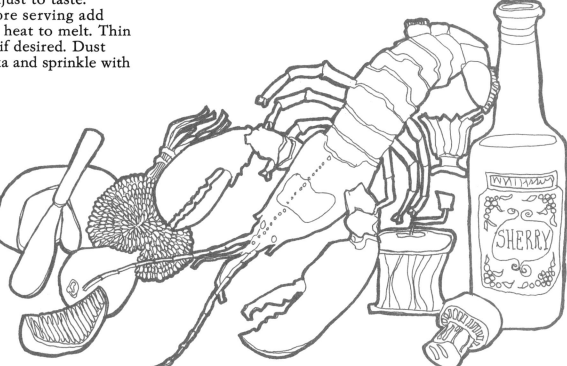

CRAB WITH PASTA

Serves 4
1 pound flaked crab meat
1/4 cup dry sherry
1 cup minced celery
3/4 cup minced onion
1/2 cup minced bell pepper
3 tablespoons butter
1 teaspoon unbleached flour
1/2 teaspoon sugar
1/2 teaspoon chili powder
2 cups half-and-half cream
    or milk
1/4 cup small seashell pasta,
    cooked al dente
Salt and white pepper to taste
1/2 teaspoon Worcestershire
    sauce
Whipped cream
Minced fresh parsley
Freshly ground pepper

Combine crab and sherry and marinate at least 1 hour.

Sauté celery, onion and bell pepper in butter until vegetables are tender. Sprinkle with flour, sugar and chili; cook and stir 3 minutes. Gradually add cream; cook and stir until smooth and slightly thickened. Add crab and sherry and pasta. Reheat without boiling and add Worcestershire sauce, salt and white pepper. Garnish with dollops of whipped cream and minced parsley. Pass the peppermill.

SHRIMP BISQUE

Serves 4 to 6
2 pounds shrimp, shelled and
    deveined
3 tablespoons butter
2 tablespoons *each* minced
    carrot, onion and celery
1 garlic clove, minced
1 bay leaf
1/4 teaspoon ground thyme
3 tablespoons minced fresh
    parsley
1 tablespoon fresh lemon juice
2 cups chicken stock
1 cup fish stock
1 cup half-and-half cream
1/2 cup heavy cream
Salt, white pepper, Tabasco
    sauce and Worcestershire
    sauce to taste
1/2 cup dry white wine
Minced fresh dill

Mince 1-1/2 pounds of the shrimp and set aside. Melt butter until bubbly and over high heat sauté the rest of the shrimp with carrot, onion, celery and garlic 5 to 8 minutes, stirring constantly. Do not overcook. Remove shrimp, dice and reserve.

Combine minced shrimp, bay leaf, thyme, parsley, lemon juice and stocks. Cover, bring to boil, lower heat and simmer 45 minutes, stirring occasionally.

Discard bay leaf. Purée and reheat with creams and reserved shrimp. Adjust seasonings with salt, pepper, Tabasco and Worcestershire sauce. Just before serving add wine. Serve with a generous sprinkling of dill.

CLAM CHOWDER

Serves 6

1 cup minced green onions, leeks and/or onions
1 garlic clove, minced
1/4 pound salt pork, diced
3 tablespoons butter
3 cups brown chicken stock
2-1/2 cups diced baking potatoes
1 bay leaf
1/4 teaspoon ground thyme
1/8 teaspoon ground allspice
1/4 teaspoon black pepper
3 dozen clams, shucked, and their liquor
1 cup bottled clam juice
1-1/2 cups half-and-half cream
1/2 cup heavy cream
Salt to taste
Butter, cut into bits
Paprika
Slivered green onions

Sauté onions, garlic and salt pork in butter until onions are soft. Add stock, potatoes, bay leaf, thyme, allspice and pepper. Cover, bring to boil, lower heat and simmer 10 minutes. Potatoes should remain crisp. Remove bay leaf.

Mince clams, add to soup with their liquor, juice and the creams, and reheat without boiling. Season with salt and adjust to taste. Stir in butter bits and sprinkle with paprika and slivered green onions.

VARIATIONS For garlic lovers, finely minced raw garlic sprinkled on top of soup just before serving adds a real zest.

Substitute 3 cans (7-1/2 ounces *each*) minced clams and their liquor for fresh clams and bottled juice.

CLAM AND LEEK SOUP

Serves 6 to 8

2 cups minced leeks (white and some green)
1/4 cup *each* minced celery and onion
2 garlic cloves, minced
3 tablespoons minced carrot
4 tablespoons butter and/or rendered chicken fat
4 cups dark beef stock
1-1/2 cups diced potatoes
1 can (7-1/2 ounce) minced clams and liquor
1 can (7-1/2 ounce) chopped clams and liquor
1 cup half-and-half cream
Salt, white pepper, cayenne pepper, freshly grated lemon peel and celery salt to taste
Butter, cut into bits
Finely minced fresh parsley and garlic
Paprika

Sauté leeks, celery, onion, garlic and carrot in butter until leeks are soft. Add stock and potatoes, cover, bring to a boil, lower heat and simmer until potatoes are tender. Purée.

Combine potato mixture with clams and add cream. Reheat, but do not boil. Add seasonings to taste. Stir in butter bits. Sprinkle with a generous amount of parsley, garlic and paprika.

CREAMY CLAM WITH SPINACH

Serves 4

3 tablespoons minced onion
2 tablespoons butter
1 tablespoon minced shallots
1 garlic clove, minced
2 bunches spinach, chopped
1/4 teaspoon black pepper
1/2 teaspoon seafood seasoning
2 cans (7-1/2 ounces *each*) minced clams and liquor
1 to 2 tablespoons fresh lemon juice
2 cups half-and-half cream
Freshly grated Parmesan cheese

Sauté onion in butter until soft. Add shallots and garlic and cook 3 minutes. Add spinach, pepper and seafood seasoning; cover and cook until spinach is tender.

Purée half of spinach mixture with 1 can clams. Remove to saucepan and repeat with remaining clams and spinach mixture.

Combine purée with lemon juice and cream; reheat, but do not boil. Adjust seasonings to taste and serve with a sprinkling of Parmesan cheese.

VARIATION Season with freshly grated nutmeg. Serve very cold in chilled bowls, garnished with hard-cooked egg slices, lemon slices and minced fresh parsley.

CLAM AND MUSHROOM SOUP

Serves 4

2 medium leeks, thinly sliced
  (white and some green)
1 large garlic clove,
  minced
2 teaspoons minced fresh
  tarragon
2 tablespoons butter and/or
  rendered chicken fat
1 tablespoon unbleached
  flour
2 cans (7-1/2 ounces *each*)
  minced clams
1/2 cup dry vermouth
1/3 cup mushroom concentrate
  (page 14)
3/4 pound mushrooms, sliced
Salt and white pepper to taste
1/3 cup sour cream, or to taste
Minced fresh parsley and/or
  chives
Sour cream
Garlic or cheese croutons

Cook leeks, garlic and tarragon in butter, covered, until leeks are soft. Sprinkle with flour; cook, stirring, 3 minutes. Drain clam liquor into a 2-cup measure, adding water to measure 2 cups. Gradually stir into leek mixture with vermouth and mushroom concentrate. Add mushrooms, salt and pepper. Cover, bring to gentle boil, lower heat and simmer 10 minutes or until mushrooms are tender. Add sour cream and reserved clams. Reheat and adjust seasonings. Sprinkle with parsley and garnish with dollops of sour cream. Pass the croutons.

CREAM OF CLAM BROTH

Serves 6

2-2/3 cups fresh clam juice,
   or 3 bottles (7 ounces *each*)
   clam juice
1 cup water
1 tablespoon chicken stock
   base
1-1/2 cups half-and-half
   cream
3 tablespoons minced shallots
2 tablespoons butter
2 tablespoons unbleached
   flour
Tabasco sauce, white pepper
   and salt to taste
1/3 cup dry white wine
Butter, cut into bits
Paprika
Finely minced green onion
   tops

---

*Shallots have a unique flavor.
Try not to substitute.*

Combine clam juice, water, stock base and cream; heat without boiling. Sauté shallots in butter until soft, sprinkle with flour and cook, stirring, 3 minutes. Gradually add clam mixture; stir and cook until smooth and slightly thickened. Season with Tabasco, pepper and salt, and adjust to taste.

Just before serving, add wine, swirl in butter bits and sprinkle with finely minced green onion tops.

VARIATION Ladle into ovenproof bowls, top with whipped cream and broil to brown. Sprinkle with minced fresh chives.

POACHED FISH IN BROTH

Serves 6

6 cups fish stock
1 tablespoon minced fresh
   tarragon
1/2 cup dry white wine
1 tablespoon fresh lemon juice
3 haddock fillets (or other
   firm fish)
Aioli Sauce or Anchovy-Egg
   Sauce (page 172)
Lemon wedges
Minced fresh parsley

Bring stock, tarragon and wine to boil. Lower heat, add lemon juice and fish and boil *gently* 7 to 10 minutes or until tender. Do not overcook.

Place half a fillet in each soup bowl, ladle soup over and top with a tablespoon of sauce.

Garnish with lemon wedges and sprinkle with parsley.

CURRIED TURKEY SOUP

Serves 6
3 or 4 slices lean bacon, minced
1 cup chopped onions
3/4 cup diced tart apple
1/2 teaspoon minced garlic
2 teaspoons curry powder
1/4 teaspoon ground cardamom
1/2 teaspoon salt
6 cups turkey stock
3 egg yolks, beaten
1 cup buttermilk
1 to 1-1/2 cups cubed cooked turkey
Minced fresh parsley
Slivered almonds, browned in butter

When recipes call for rice flour, don't confuse it with sweet (or glutinous) rice flour.

Cook bacon until crisp. Remove with slotted spoon and set aside. Sauté onions, apple and garlic in drippings until onions are soft. Sprinkle with curry powder and cardamom; cook, stirring, 3 minutes. Add salt and stock, cover, bring to gentle boil, lower heat and simmer 30 minutes. Purée.

Beat together yolks and buttermilk and add to purée with turkey. Bring just to boil, adjust seasonings and sprinkle generously with parsley. Pass reserved bacon bits and almonds.

SWEETBREAD SOUP

Serves 6
2 or 3 pairs veal sweetbreads
2 medium onions, thinly sliced
3 tablespoons sliced leek (white only)
2 carrots, thinly sliced
2 tablespoons rendered chicken fat and/or butter
2 tablespoons rice flour
8 cups brown chicken stock
1 bay leaf
1 sprig *each* thyme and oregano
1 teaspoon salt
1/4 teaspoon white pepper
3 potatoes, scrubbed and sliced
1 small cabbage, shredded
Minced fresh chives
Paprika

Cover sweetbreads with ice water and refrigerate 30 minutes. Trim, slice and set aside.

Brown onions, leek and carrots in chicken fat and sprinkle with flour. Cook, stirring, 2 minutes. Add stock, herbs, salt and pepper and reserved sweetbreads.

Cover, bring to boil, lower heat and simmer 10 minutes. Add potatoes, bring back to boil and simmer 10 minutes. Add cabbage and cook over medium heat 5 minutes. Discard herbs, adjust seasonings and sprinkle with chives and paprika.

VARIATION Add 1-1/2 cups peeled and chopped ripe tomatoes with cabbage.

Oriental Soups

Balance the yang and yin of textures
With crisp morsels, soft delicacies, sauces, soups
And the finest pearly rice.
Let lingering tastes bring only pleasant memories.
                                        —T'sai-shuh

Volumes could be written about fascinating Oriental soups never encountered in restaurants. This I discovered under the tutelage of three experts, one Chinese, two Japanese. Especially interesting were the trips to Oriental markets to purchase fuzzy melon, dried fish stomach, seaweed, superior fresh seafoods and myriad other strange or familiar ingredients. Most Americans of European descent are just beginning to appreciate that weird (to them) odors of an Oriental market are far removed from the fragrant broths to be sipped from delicate bowls or centered on the table for individual ladling.

A common misconception is to think of foods of the Orient in terms of mostly Chinese or Japanese. Korea, Indonesia, India, Sri Lanka and other Far East countries have many tasty foods and flavors, too.

For those fortunate enough to live in an area with Oriental neighborhoods, it's easy to build up a supply of dried items for variety in many dishes. They keep indefinitely and need only to be thoroughly washed before using, and sometimes soaked in warm water to soften.

Dried forest mushrooms must *always* be soaked. Cover with lukewarm water for 10 minutes or more, rinse, dry and use as recipe directs. For Japanese recipes, sprinkle with a little sugar when soaking. The soaking water can be reserved and used as part of the liquid called for in the recipe or can be added to stocks.

The light soy is less salty than the heavier, dark variety and is to be used in all recipes.

For the more complicated Oriental soups, soaking, dicing and other preliminary processing of ingredients should be done well ahead of time. You'll note that some of the soups can be prepared the day before. Refrigerate, and reheat just before serving—a great help to cooks who are also hosts or hostesses.

CREAMY SRI LANKAN SOUP WITH CURRY PUFFS

Serves 6

1-1/2 cups diced tart apples
3 tablespoons grated onion
2 tablespoons butter
1 tablespoon unbleached flour
1 to 2 teaspoons curry powder
5 cups chicken stock
1/2 cup dry white wine
3 egg yolks, beaten
2 cups heavy cream
Salt and white pepper to taste
Half-and-half cream
3/4 cup minced cooked chicken or shrimp
Minced fresh chives or green onion tops
1 recipe Curry Puffs (following)

98

Sauté apples and onion in butter 10 minutes without browning. Sprinkle with flour and curry powder, cook, stirring, 3 minutes and gradually add stock and wine. Cook and stir until smooth and slightly thickened. Cover and cook gently 20 minutes. Strain and reheat.

Beat together yolks and cream, whisk in 1/2 cup hot soup and return to rest of soup. Cook and stir 3 minutes without boiling. Cool and chill.

Adjust seasonings with salt and pepper; thin with half-and-half cream if desired. Serve in chilled bowls and sprinkle with chicken or shrimp and chives. Pass the Curry Puffs.

VARIATION Serve hot, garnished with sieved hard-cooked egg and paprika.

CURRY PUFFS

Makes approximately 30
1 pound ground lean beef
3 tablespoons butter
1/4 cup minced onion
1/8 teaspoon garlic powder
1/2 to 1 teaspoon ground cumin
1 teaspoon salt
Dash *each* ground cinnamon and ginger and cayenne pepper
1/2 cup plain yoghurt
1/2 cup minced cooked potato
1 hard-cooked egg, chopped
1/2 cup raisins
1 tablespoon fresh lemon juice
One 1-pound package phyllo*
Melted butter

Sauté beef until brown, remove from pan and drain. Pour any remaining fat from pan, add butter and sauté onion until soft. Add seasonings, return meat to pan and cook and stir 3 minutes. Blend in yoghurt and simmer to absorb almost all the liquid. Add all remaining ingredients, except phyllo, mix well and cool.

When working with phyllo pastry always keep it covered with wax paper and a dampened towel to prevent it from drying out. If the layers break, don't worry, as you can "mend" them with the melted butter as you place layer on layer. Remove 4 layers at a time, spread each with melted butter using a pastry brush, and restack them. Cut into 2-1/2-inch rounds, place 1 teaspoon of filling on rounds and fold over to form a half-moon shape, crimping the edges to seal. Place on cookie sheet and repeat until all the filling is used, making about 30 puffs. Bake in a 350° oven 15 minutes or until golden.

*Phyllo pastry sheets are available in pound packages in Armenian or Greek specialty shops and in many delicatessens. I do not recommend frozen phyllo, but if none other is available be sure to let it defrost overnight in the refrigerator before using.

Any leftover pastry can be used for strudel, baklava, or even a casing for meatloaf. Wrap well and refrigerate up to 5 days.

Unbaked puffs may be frozen for up to 3 months. Defrost in the refrigerator.

SRI LANKAN CONSOMME

Serves 6

3 cups diced tart apples
3/4 cup minced onion
1 cup chopped celery leaves
3 tablespoons unsalted butter
1 to 2 teaspoons curry powder
4 cups Beef Consommé
   (page 20)
3 cups half-and-half cream

Sauté apples, onion and celery leaves in butter 10 minutes; do not brown. Sprinkle with curry and cook, stirring, 3 minutes.

Add the consommé, bring to boil, lower heat and simmer, uncovered, 15 minutes. Strain and adjust seasonings. Add cream and reheat.

NOTE This soup may also be served cold.

INDONESIAN BEEF BROTH WITH MEATBALLS

Serves 6

6 cups beef stock
2 bay leaves
1 teaspoon laos*
1 teaspoon serehpoeder*
1/2 teaspoon garlic powder
1 rib celery, thinly sliced
   on diagonal
1 teaspoon peanut oil
1 recipe Meatballs (following)
Salt and black pepper to taste
Slivered green onions
*See glossary

Combine stock, bay leaves, laos, serehpoeder and garlic powder. Cover, bring to boil, lower heat and simmer gently 30 minutes to blend flavors. Remove bay leaves.

Cook celery in oil, covered, 10 minutes. Add to broth, bring to gentle boil and drop in as many meatballs as desired. Cook 8 to 10 minutes and adjust seasonings with salt and pepper. Serve with a generous amount of slivered green onions.

MEATBALLS

1/4 pound *each* ground
   round steak and lean pork
   butt
1/2 cup riced boiled potatoes
1/2 teaspoon soy sauce
1/4 teaspoon salt
1/8 teaspoon *each* ground
   mace and freshly grated
   nutmeg
1 tablespoon cornstarch

Mix together all ingredients thoroughly. Form balls the size of marbles and chill at least 1 hour. Can be cooked in soup, as above, or in boiling salted water.

INDONESIAN CHICKEN BROTH

Serves 6
6 cups chicken stock
2 bay leaves
1 slice ginger root
1/2 teaspoon laos*
1/2 teaspoon serehpoeder*
1/2 teaspoon boemboe
   godok*
1/2 teaspoon garlic powder
1 cup julienned raw chicken
2 ribs celery, thinly sliced
   on diagonal
1/2 cup diced onion
2 teaspoons peanut oil
2 to 3 ounces bean-thread
   noodles*, soaked in water
   to cover 10 minutes,
   drained and cut into 4-inch
   lengths
Slivered green onions
*See glossary

Combine stock, bay leaves, ginger and seasonings. Cover, bring to boil, lower heat and simmer 30 minutes. Add chicken last 10 minutes. Remove bay leaves and ginger.

Cook celery and onion in oil, covered, 10 minutes. Add to broth, bring to boil and cook 5 minutes. Add bean-thread noodles and boil 2 to 3 minutes. Adjust seasonings to taste.

Serve with a generous amount of slivered green onions.

To soften dried mushrooms, soak in warm water 5 to 10 minutes, then drain and use as directed. Always save the soaking water for adding to soups and stocks for extra flavor.

ORIENTAL CRAB AND CORN BISQUE

Serves 8
8 cups Basic Chinese Chicken
   or Pork Broth
6 fresh mushrooms, sliced, or
   6 dried forest mushrooms,
   softened and slivered
1 white onion, sliced
2 cups white cream-style corn
Sugar, soy sauce and black
   pepper to taste
1 to 1-1/2 cups flaked crab
   meat
2 eggs, beaten

Simmer stock, mushrooms and onion, covered, 30 minutes, adding corn last 10 minutes. Adjust seasonings with sugar, soy and pepper and add crab and reheat.

Bring to slow boil, gradually drizzle in eggs and stir with fork so eggs form long, slender strands.

THAI SOUP WITH LEMON

Serves 6 to 8
3/4 pound shrimp
1/2 pound fish heads and
   scraps
2 bay leaves
6 black peppercorns, lightly
   crushed
1 onion, sliced
Tops of 4 green onions,
   chopped
2 dried red chili peppers,
   crushed
3 tablespoons fresh lemon
   juice
1 tablespoon freshly grated
   lemon peel
6 cups water
1/2 pound lean pork, cut into
   julienne
1 raw chicken breast, cut into
   julienne
1/2 pound firm white fish
   fillet, cut into 1-inch squares
Fish sauce or fish soy*
Fresh lemon juice
Salt
*See glossary

Shell and devein shrimp, dice and reserve. Combine shells, fish heads and scraps, bay leaves, peppercorns, onion, green onion tops, chili peppers, lemon juice and peel and water. Cover, bring to boil, lower heat and simmer 30 minutes; skim off any scum that rises to surface. Strain and reheat.

Add pork and cook 10 minutes; add chicken and cook 5 minutes. Bring back to boil, add fish squares and cook gently 5 more minutes. Add shrimp dice, bring back to boil and remove from heat.

Season to taste with fish sauce, lemon juice and salt.

THE ORIENTAL FIREPOT

Strangers become friends and friends get friendlier around a firepot soup. The spectacular shiny brass firepot filled with glowing charcoal is designed specifically for this soup, though not absolutely necessary. Electric casserole cookers or pretty kettles over braziers make suitable substitutes.

The seafood, poultry, meat, vegetables, garnishes and seasonings listed are just a few of many you may wish to try. Arrange them attractively on platters and trays where they'll be easily accessible to you and your guests. Surround the pot with individual plates and bowls. The broth should be gently simmering. Everyone picks up his chopsticks and cooks morsels in the broth. Keeping track of whose morsels are whose can be quite a game.

Small individual wire sieves are best for retrieving the morsels at their parboiled, crunchy best. The retrieved delicacies may be eaten with chopsticks or sandwiched in pieces of iceberg lettuce. It's advisable to provide Oriental soup spoons, too, for sipping the broth later.

If desired, each guest may break a small egg into his bowl, beat it lightly and dip hot morsels into it before or after seasoning.

When everyone has had his fill of morsels, add bean-thread noodles and two beaten eggs to the broth; let simmer to set eggs and serve. Or omit beaten eggs and ladle hot soup over eggs left in bowls.

8 cups Basic Chinese Chicken Broth
8 scallops, halved
8 shrimp, shelled, deveined and halved lengthwise
1 small abalone, cut in julienne
1/2 pound fillet of sole, cubed
Other firm raw fish in season
1 chicken breast, cut in julienne
1 pork fillet, cut in julienne
1/2 pound top sirloin beef, thinly sliced
3 chicken gizzards, scored and thinly sliced
1 bunch small spinach leaves
1 small Chinese cabbage, leaves separated
1 bunch watercress
4 green onions, cut into 4-inch lengths
Other vegetables in season
4 ounces bean-thread noodles*, soaked 10 minutes in water to cover, drained and cut into 6-inch lengths
Eggs

IN SMALL BOWLS
Hoisin sauce*
Prepared mustard
Slivered green onions
Toasted sesame seeds
Oyster sauce*

IN ATTRACTIVE SHAKE BOTTLES
Soy sauce
Dry sherry
Oriental-style sesame oil
White vinegar
Aji oil*
*See glossary

KOREAN SOUP WITH MANDOO

Serves 6
1/2 pound round steak, cut on diagonal into very thin slices
3 green onions, minced
2 tablespoons soy sauce
1/2 teaspoon minced garlic
1/2 teaspoon peeled and minced ginger root
1 teaspoon lightly toasted sesame seeds
1-1/2 tablespoons peanut oil
4 cups water
2 cups beef stock
1 large dried forest mushroom, softened
Salt to taste
12 pea pods, blanched 2 minutes
1 small square soybean curd, diced
1 recipe Mandoo (following)
Slivered green onions
*See glossary

Marinate meat with green onions, soy, garlic, ginger and sesame seeds at least 2 hours.

Heat oil and brown meat mixture. Add water, stock and mushroom. Cover, bring to boil, lower heat and simmer 20 minutes. Remove mushroom and cut into 12 slivers; set aside. Adjust seasoning with salt.

Arrange 2 mushroom slivers, 2 pea pods, several soybean curd dice and as many Mandoo as desired in 6 bowls. Ladle soup over and sprinkle with slivered green onions.

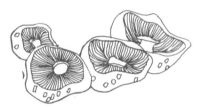

MANDOO

1/2 pound ground round steak
2 tablespoons kim chee*, drained, squeezed dry and chopped
1 tablespoon minced green onion
1/2 teaspoon finely minced ginger root
1 teaspoon lightly toasted sesame seeds
1/8 teaspoon *each* black pepper, paprika and sugar
1/2 teaspoon salt
1 teaspoon cornstarch
Wonton Skins (page 106)
*See glossary

Mix together all ingredients, except skins. Fill skins and cook in boiling salted water 5 minutes or until they rise to the surface.

Chinese Soups

Although appearance is important in Chinese cooking, and many of the foods look spectacular, flavor and texture are even more important.
- When one vegetable or meat is diced, all others in recipe should be diced whenever possible; if slivered, all slivered.
- A dash of sugar often brings out just the flavor you're looking for.
- Soy sauce will darken soup and ingredients, so if you want to keep fish, chicken and water chestnuts white, let your guests add soy.
- The Chinese like Virginia ham and it is usually available in their markets. Substitute prosciutto, sliced 1/4-inch thick.
- Ingredients can be omitted, increased or decreased in Chinese soups. Keep a varied stock on hand for exploring the possibilities.
- Ginger root need not be peeled. Just slice, wash and use to flavor.
- There is no substitute for dried tangerine peel, sometimes called dried orange peel, which can be purchased in Chinese markets.
- Rice should be long grain.

BASIC CHINESE BROTH

This broth is to be used in all Chinese soups.

2 pounds chicken or pork
   bones
8 cups water
1 or 2 slices ginger root
Dash sugar
Salt

Combine chicken and/or pork bones with water and ginger; cover, bring to boil, skim off any scum that rises to top, lower heat and simmer gently 45 minutes to 1-1/2 hours. Strain and season to taste with sugar and salt.

VARIATIONS FOR CHINESE BROTH

- Cut Chinese cabbage lengthwise in eighths. Slice crosswise 1/4 inch thick. Add to broth and simmer 5 minutes.
- Add 1 cup diced soybean curd to broth and simmer 5 minutes.
- Combine the cabbage and soybean curd in the broth.
- Add dried forest mushrooms, softened and slivered, to broth and simmer 20 minutes.
- Cut core end of mustard greens in 1/2-inch slices; cut green part into 2-inch slices. Wash thoroughly in several changes of water. Drain and add to boiling pork stock that has simmered with an extra slice of ginger root. Bring to boil and cook 5 minutes. Remove ginger and adjust seasonings.

WONTON SOUP

Serves 6

6 cups Basic Chinese Chicken
  or Pork Broth
1 strand dried turnip greens*,
  washed to remove sand
  (optional)
1 dried tangerine peel*,
  soaked 10 minutes in water
  to cover and drained
4 dried forest mushrooms,
  softened and slivered
Salt and soy sauce to taste
24 wontons (page 108)
Chinese parsley sprigs
*See glossary

Simmer broth with turnip
greens, tangerine peel and
mushrooms for 30 minutes.
Remove greens and tangerine
peel. Season with salt and
soy. Keep hot.

   In separate saucepan cook
wontons in salted boiling
water 4 to 5 minutes, or until
they rise to top; do not boil
too hard. Then cook 1 more
minute and drain well.

   Remove wontons with slotted
spoon and place 4 in each of
6 bowls. Fill bowls with hot
soup and garnish with Chinese parsley.

WAH WONTON SOUP

Serves 6 to 8

6 cups broth, prepared as for
  Wonton Soup (preceding)
3 chicken gizzards, scored
  and thinly sliced
3 chicken hearts, sliced
1/2 cup slivered bamboo
  shoots
3 chicken livers, halved or
  quartered
3 medium squid, cleaned,
  halved lengthwise and
  thinly sliced
1/4 pound whole pea pods, or
  1 small bunch bok choy,
  coarsely chopped and well
  washed
6 shrimp, shelled, deveined
  and halved lengthwise
24 wontons (page 108)

Bring simmered broth to boil,
add gizzards and hearts and
cook 3 minutes. Add bamboo
shoots, livers, squid and vegetable; bring back to boil and
cook 2 minutes. Add shrimp,
bring just to boil and remove
from heat. Add wontons, as
in Wonton Soup.

VARIATION Add pieces of cooked
slivered pork and/or chicken,
and for a main meal, more
wontons.

WONTON SKINS

Ready-made wonton skins, in
one-pound packages of squares
or rounds, are sold in many
markets other than Oriental.
There are about 80 in each
package, depending upon how
thin they've been rolled. If
well wrapped, they may be
frozen, but the skins dry out
more readily and become difficult to manipulate.

   Homemade skins are equally
as good, but without proper
equipment it is difficult to
roll them thin enough. The
recipe follows in case you
can't find them in your market.

   If you have leftover uncooked filled wontons, they
can be frozen for up to one
week. Then defrost, and add
to soup, or deep-fry for an
accompaniment.

   If you have leftover wonton
skins, drop a few at a time
into oil, deep-fry until golden,
drain on paper toweling and
sprinkle with powdered sugar.
Serve as cookies for dessert.

Makes approximately 40
1/2 cup hot water
1 teaspoon *each* corn oil and
  salt
2 cups unbleached flour

Combine water, oil and salt;
quickly add flour, mix well
and knead until smooth. Roll
into 3 or 4 ropes 1/2 inch in
diameter. Wrap each rope in
waxed paper and refrigerate
30 minutes. Working with 1
rope at a time, cut off 1/2-
inch pieces and roll as thinly
as possible into squares or
rounds. Stack, keeping covered, and repeat with remaining ropes.

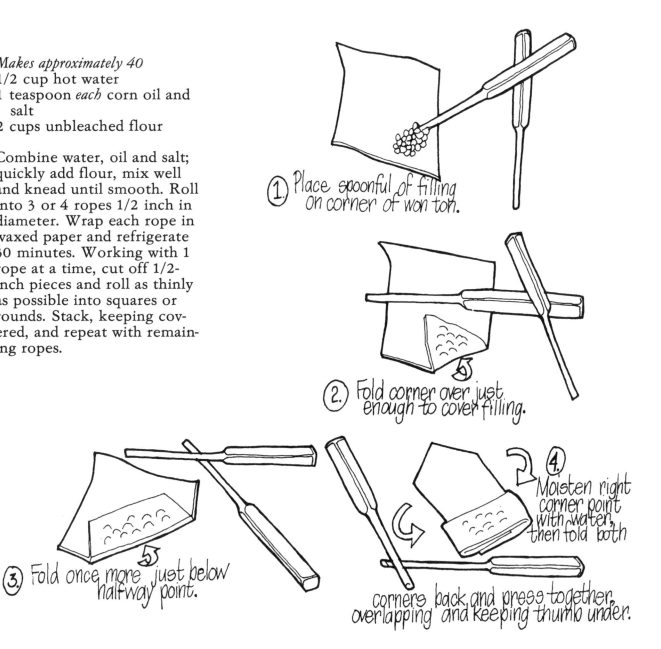

1. Place spoonful of filling on corner of won ton.

2. Fold corner over just enough to cover filling.

3. Fold once more just below halfway point.

4. Moisten right corner point with water, then fold both corners back and press together, overlapping and keeping thumb under.

SHRIMP WONTON FILLING

1 pound shrimp, shelled, deveined and ground or finely minced
1/2 cup minced water chestnuts
1 tablespoon minced green onion
1/2 teaspoon minced garlic
1/4 teaspoon salt
1 teaspoon *each* soy sauce and dry sherry
1 tablespoon cornstarch

Mix together all ingredients thoroughly and fill wonton squares as directed.

Use thinly sliced sunchokes, cauliflower cores or broccoli stems in place of water chestnuts.

PORK WONTON FILLING

3/4 pound minced lean pork butt
2 tablespoons minced green onion
1 garlic clove, minced
2 teaspoons dry sherry
1 tablespoon soy sauce
1/2 teaspoon salt

Mix together all ingredients thoroughly and fill wonton squares as directed.

PORK AND SHRIMP WONTON FILLING

1/2 pound ground lean pork butt
1/2 pound shrimp, shelled, deveined and ground or finely minced
1 tablespoon minced Chinese parsley
3 green onions and tops, minced
1 tablespoon soy sauce
8 water chestnuts, minced
1/4 teaspoon salt
1 tablespoon cornstarch
1 egg, beaten

Mix together all ingredients thoroughly and fill wonton squares as directed.

BEEF WONTON FILLING

1 pound ground lean beef
2 tablespoons minced green onion
1 garlic clove, minced
2 teaspoons dry sherry
1 tablespoon *each* cornstarch and soy sauce
1/2 teaspoon salt
1/4 teaspoon freshly grated ginger root

Mix together all ingredients thoroughly. Place 1 rounded teaspoon of filling in center of round wonton skin, fold over to make half-moon shape and crimp edges, using water to seal.

DICED WINTER MELON SOUP

Serves 8

8 cups Basic Chinese Chicken or Pork Broth
2 pounds winter melon, washed, peeled and diced
6 large dried forest mushrooms, softened and diced
One 1-inch piece dried tangerine peel*, soaked in water to cover 10 minutes and drained
1/2 cup *each* diced water chestnuts and bamboo shoots
1 chicken breast, skinned, boned and diced
Salt
1/2 cup slivered Virginia ham
Chinese parsley sprigs
*See glossary

Combine broth, winter melon, mushrooms, tangerine peel, water chestnuts and bamboo shoots in large kettle; cover, bring to boil, lower heat and simmer gently 1 hour, adding chicken last 10 minutes. Discard tangerine peel and adjust seasonings with salt. Garnish with ham and Chinese parsley.

VARIATION Add 1/2 cup shelled green peas with the chicken. Add 2 tablespoons dry sherry just before serving.

WINTER MELON POND SOUP

Instead of using diced winter melon, the broth, mushrooms, tangerine peel, water chestnuts, bamboo shoots and chicken are cooked in the whole melon and the soup is served from the melon—a spectacular dish!

Buy an evenly shaped melon, about 10 pounds in weight; cut off the top one-quarter of the melon and set aside. Scrape out the pulp and seeds and set the melon in a bowl that just fits its circumference. Make a string "harness" around bowl and melon, or wrap in double-strength cheesecloth, for easy handling and set on a rack in a large kettle. Fill the melon with stock and ingredients, reserving any extra stock for serving on side or for future use. Put top on melon and pour boiling water into kettle, filling seven-eighths full. Cover kettle and steam gently 3 hours. Lift melon and bowl from kettle, remove harness or cheesecloth, discard tangerine peel, and serve, scooping out some of the flesh with each serving.

SIZZLING RICE SOUP

The sizzle's the secret; don't muff it. Cooking rice the Chinese way is essential.

Serves 6
1 cup well-washed long-grain white rice
1-1/2 cups water
8 cups Basic Chinese Chicken Broth
1 cup sliced canned button mushrooms
1/4 cup sliced water chestnuts
1/2 cup diagonally sliced bamboo shoots
1 chicken breast, skinned, boned and cut in julienne
2 cups shredded lettuce or Chinese cabbage
Corn oil for deep-frying

Combine rice and water in heavy frying pan and let stand at least 1 hour. Bring to boil, uncovered, over high heat, lower heat slightly and boil until water evaporates. Cover with a tight lid, reduce heat to its lowest and cook 1-1/2 hours, or until the crust that has formed can be removed easily from pan. Refrigerate 1 hour or more and then break into bite-size pieces.

Bring stock to boil, add mushrooms, water chestnuts, bamboo shoots and chicken. Cook 10 minutes, add lettuce and bring back to boil. Cook 1 minute.

While soup is cooking, deep-fry rice pieces in corn oil until golden. Drain on paper toweling and keep hot in a casserole in a 375° oven.

The timing is important—both the fried rice and the soup should be very hot. Bring the casserole to the table and let your guests watch you pour the soup over it and enjoy the sizzle. Also the taste!

CHINESE OXTAIL-BLACK BEAN SOUP

Serves 8 to 10
1 whole lean oxtail (about 1-1/2 pounds), cut into 1-1/2-inch lengths (large pieces halved) and blanched
8 cups water
1 dried tangerine peel, soaked in water to cover 10 minutes and drained
8 to 10 dried forest mushrooms, softened
8 to 10 jujubes*, washed
1 slice ginger root
3/4 teaspoon salt
1/2 teaspoon sugar
1 cup dried Oriental black beans*, washed, blanched, rinsed and then soaked in water to cover 3 to 4 hours
*See glossary

Combine oxtails, water, tangerine peel, mushrooms, jujubes, ginger, salt and sugar. Cover, bring to boil, lower heat and simmer 1-1/2 hours. Add beans and cook 30 minutes to 1 hour longer, or until beans are tender but still hold their shape. Remove tangerine peel and adjust seasonings to taste.

VARIATION Add 1 teaspoon whiskey or dry sherry to each bowl before ladling in soup.

CHINESE CHICKEN WHISKEY SOUP

This is served to Chinese mothers after their babies are born to help them regain their strength. It is best when made a day ahead and reheated. The needles add an unusual sweet flavor.

Serves 6
1-1/2 pounds chicken wings or other cut of choice
2 ounces dried black fungus*, soaked in warm water to cover 10 minutes
1/2 cup dried needles*, soaked in cold water to cover 5 minutes
3 tablespoons corn oil
1/2 teaspoon salt
5 to 8 slices ginger root
10 small dried forest mushrooms, softened
1 cup blanched raw Virginia peanuts
3 cups boiling water
1/4 cup bourbon
*See glossary

Remove tips from wings and reserve for future stock. Cut wings at joints and set aside.

Cut out any hard membrane in fungus and pull apart into bite-size pieces. Set aside. Tie each needle into a knot and set aside.

Heat oil, sprinkle with salt and cook and stir ginger 2 minutes over high heat. Add wings and brown. Add fungus, mushrooms and peanuts; cook and stir over high heat 1 minute.

Add boiling water and bourbon, cover, bring to boil, lower heat and simmer 20 minutes, adding needles last 10 minutes of cooking. Just before serving, skim off surface fat.

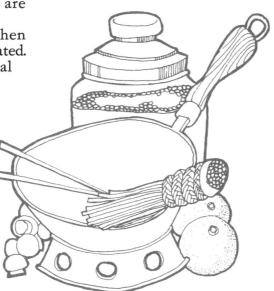

JOOK OR CONGEE
Chinese Thick Rice Soup

Never as a first course—good as a main meal, or for a late supper or breakfast. Bland and interesting, this cold-weather soup can be made ahead and reheated again and again.

Serves 8

8 cups turkey broth, made according to directions for Basic Chinese Broth
8 dried forest mushrooms, softened and slivered
1 large piece dried tangerine peel*, soaked 10 minutes in water to cover and drained
1/2 dried turnip green*, well washed and sliced
1 cup long-grain white rice (unwashed)
2-1/2 cups boiling water
3 or 4 sheets dried sheet soybean curd, broken into bite-size pieces
1 to 2 cups diced cooked turkey
3 lop chiang*, sliced on the diagonal
Oriental-style sesame oil, soy sauce and salt to taste
Slivered green onions
Chinese parsley sprigs
Small raw fish slices
*See glossary

Combine broth, mushrooms, tangerine peel and turnip green and simmer while making rice.

Over high heat, cook rice in boiling water, stirring occasionally. Keep a tea kettle of boiling water ready to add as needed. After 15 minutes lower heat slightly. Rice should cook until it is completely broken up and gooey, 30 to 40 minutes.

Add rice to broth and cook, stirring occasionally, for 1 hour, or until broth resembles a gruel. Last 15 minutes add soybean curd; last 10 minutes add turkey and sausages. Keep adding boiling water as needed. Adjust seasonings with sesame oil, soy and salt. Pass bowls of slivered green onions and Chinese parsley sprigs. Serve with raw fish slices to dip into hot soup.

Japanese Soups

Delicacy of flavor, beautiful and artistic garnishes, graceful bowls and ritualistic serving characterize Japanese soups, which are second only to rice in culinary importance. Odd numbers are considered lucky in Japan; even numbers unlucky. Thus the Japanese place odd numbers of each type of morsel in the bowl and odd numbers of people are seated around the table. Bowls are sold in sets of five, not four or six.

The three major types of Japanese soup are suimono, clear, served at the beginning of the meal, miso, which is thickened with crushed and fermented soybeans, served toward the end of a meal or for breakfast, and sumashi-shiru, a main-meal soup like either of the former, only with higher proportions of solids, and served along with rice.

Dashi is the base of all three types. The hot soup often serves to heat the morsels, so Japanese soup bowls are always sold with lids to keep the soup very hot.

SUIMONO
Basic Dashi

DASHI #1
6-inch by 2-inch piece kombu*
6 cups water
1-1/2 cups katsuobushi*
1/8 teaspoon sugar
1/2 teaspoon salt
*See glossary

Break kombu into several pieces, combine with rest of ingredients, bring to boil and cook rapidly 3 minutes. Do not overcook. Strain and reserve kombu and katsuobushi for making Dashi #2.

DASHI #2
Repeat Dashi #1 recipe reusing reserved kombu and katsuobushi and adding an additional 1/2 cup katsuobushi. Boil 5 minutes. This increases the flavor. Strain.

VARIATIONS

• In salted water parboil 1 shrimp (cleaned, tail left on) and 3 pea pods per person. Place in bowl, add dashi and garnish with tiny lemon peel strip.
• Boil 1 or 3 clams per person in dashi until they open. Garnish with minced chives or green onion tops.
• Place 1 or 3 small squares raw fillet of sole or striped bass in bowl. Pour hot dashi over and garnish with tiny lemon peel strip.

• In salted water, parboil slices of fresh mushroom and somen (thin noodles); cut somen into 6-inch lengths and tie 5 strands together with a blanched green onion top. Place 3 slices of mushroom and 1 tied somen in each bowl. Pour hot dashi over. Garnish with watercress.
• Place 3 small tofu cubes, 3 small precooked or raw vegetable cubes, and 1 tiny sliver of cooked chicken in each bowl. Pour hot dashi over.
• Place 5 name-take*, drained, in each bowl. Pour hot dashi over and garnish with a tiny carrot curl.
• Soak matsutakefu* in water just to soften. Place 1 in each bowl and pour hot dashi over. Serve immediately.
• Can always add sake—1 tablespoon per 2 cups dashi. Pass a bottle of aji oil* for guests who like theirs hot.
*See glossary

DASHI WITH UDON

Serves 5

1/2 chicken breast, skinned, boned and cut into 15 small julienne strips
1 teaspoon soy sauce
1/2 teaspoon sake or dry sherry
Dash sugar
2 dried forest mushrooms, softened and cut into 15 slivers
5 water chestnuts, each cut into 5 slices
5-1/2 cups Dashi #2
1/4 pound fresh udon (thick wheat noodles)
6 cups hot water
Soy sauce to taste
5 tiny spinach leaves
5 tiny slivers of raw carrot
5 tiny strips of lemon peel

Marinate chicken strips in soy, sake and sugar 15 minutes. Combine with mushroom slivers, water chestnut slices and 1/2 cup of the dashi. Bring to boil and cook, covered, 10 minutes. Remove cover and let liquid boil away. Set aside and keep warm.

Cover udon with 4 cups of the hot water, bring to boil and add rest of water. Bring back to boil, cook 1 minute, drain and rinse with cold water. Shake colander to remove as much water as possible.

Heat remaining 5 cups dashi, adjust seasonings with soy, and reheat with udon.

Place 3 pieces of chicken, 3 mushroom slivers and 5 slices of water chestnut into each of 5 bowls.

Ladle dashi and udon into bowls and garnish with spinach, carrot and lemon peel.

DASHI WITH CHICKEN BALLS

Serves 7

4 dried forest mushrooms, softened and cut into 21 small slivers
1 teaspoon soy sauce
1/2 teaspoon sake or dry sherry
1/4 teaspoon sugar
7 cups Dashi #1
Salt and soy sauce to taste
1 package age*, cut in thirds
1 recipe Chicken Balls (following)
7 tiny lemon peel strips
7 small watercress sprigs

Simmer mushroom slivers in mushroom soaking water, soy, sake and sugar 10 minutes.

Bring dashi to boil and adjust seasonings to taste with salt and soy.

In each of 7 bowls place 3 mushroom slivers, 3 Chicken Balls and 3 pieces of age. Ladle hot dashi over and garnish with lemon peel and watercress sprigs.

CHICKEN BALLS

1/2 pound chicken breast, skinned, boned and finely minced
1 egg white
1 tablespoon cornstarch
1 teaspoon salt
2 tablespoons mashed cooked peas
1/4 cup bean sprouts, blanched, squeezed dry and minced
1 teaspoon sake or dry sherry
1 teaspoon soy sauce

Mix together all ingredients, form into 21 balls, and steam over gently boiling water 10 minutes.

SHRIMP BALL SOUP

Serves 5
3 cups Dashi #1
2 cups water
2 green onions, cut in 2-inch
  lengths on the diagonal
1 teaspoon soy sauce
1 recipe Shrimp Balls
  (following)
Salt

Combine dashi, water, green
onions and soy; bring to boil
and add balls. Cook until
balls rise to surface.
  Adjust seasonings with salt.

SHRIMP BALLS

1 pound shrimp, shelled,
  deveined and finely minced
1/4 teaspoon freshly grated
  ginger root
1 tablespoon shiromiso*
1 tablespoon cornstarch
*See glossary

Mix together all ingredients
and form into small balls.

BUTAGIRU

Serves 5
6 cups Chinese Pork Broth
2 medium yellow onions, cut in eighths or sixteenths
3/4 pound lean pork butt, diced
1 tablespoon soy sauce
Salt
Slivered green onions or watercress leaves

Combine all ingredients, except salt and green onions, and simmer, covered, 1 hour. Adjust seasonings with salt and garnish with slivered green onions.

Try growing your own watercress or curlycress in a shady spot with lots of waer. They reseed themselves and the young plants make excellent garnishes.

MISOSHIRU

Serves 3
3 cups Dashi #2
1/3 cup shiromiso or akamiso*
Salt
Soy sauce
Lemon peel
Minced fresh chives
Aji oil*
*See glossary

Bring dashi to boil. Put miso in a small 1/4-inch-mesh sieve, place bottom of sieve in boiling dashi and press miso through sieve with a wooden spoon. Adjust to taste with more miso, salt and soy sauce. Garnish with lemon peel and chives. Pass aji oil.

VARIATIONS
● Add 1/2 to 1 cup finely diced tofu and heat through.
● Cook diced pumpkin, sliced zucchini, cubed eggplant or potato strips in dashi before adding miso. Garnish with tiny watercress sprigs.
● Add bits of bean-thread noodles*, soaked first to soften.
● See dashi variations.
*See glossary

MISOSHIRU WITH CHICKEN AND VEGETABLES

Serves 7
7 cups Dashi #2
1/4 cup *each* slivered chicken, carrots and pea pods
2 tablespoons chopped gobo*
1/2 cup diced potatoes
2/3 cup miso*
Salt, soy sauce and shichimi* pepper to taste
Slivered green onions
*See glossary

Bring dashi to boil, add chicken and vegetables and cook until just tender-crisp.
Add miso as directed in Misoshiru (preceding), heat and blend; adjust seasonings to taste with salt, soy sauce and shichimi.
Garnish with slivered green onions.

CHAWAN MUSHI

Serves 7

7 medium dried forest mushrooms, sprinkled with 1/2
teaspoon sugar and softened
in 1/2 cup water
7 bamboo shoot tips, cut
into thirds
7 water chestnuts, each cut
into 5 slices
1 tablespoon soy sauce
1/2 teaspoon sugar
1 tablespoon mirin*

1 large chicken breast,
skinned and boned
1 teaspoon soy sauce
1/2 teaspoon salt

7 shrimp, shelled with tail
left intact and deveined
1/8 teaspoon salt
2 tablespoons sake or dry
sherry

7 gingko nuts
1 package kamaboko*, sliced

4 eggs
2-1/4 cups Dashi #1
1 tablespoon soy sauce
1 teaspoon sugar
1/2 teaspoon salt

7 tiny lemon peel strips
7 small watercress sprigs
*See glossary

Cut softened mushrooms into
thirds; combine with mushroom soaking water, bamboo
tips and water chestnuts. Cover, bring to boil and cook 10
minutes. Add soy, sugar and
mirin; cook 5 minutes, remove lid and let liquid boil
away.

Cut chicken breast lengthwise and then cut with grain
into 35 small strips. Combine
with soy and salt.

Sprinkle shrimp with salt
and drizzle sake over to coat.
Let stand 10 minutes.

Place in 7 chawan bowls: 3
pieces mushroom, 3 pieces
bamboo, 5 slices water chestnuts, 5 strips chicken, 1 shrimp,
1 gingko nut, 1 slice kamaboko.

Beat eggs with chopsticks
to blend; do not allow to
foam. Add dashi, soy sauce,
sugar and salt and heat *slightly*.
Ladle into bowls, cover bowls,
place in steamer and steam
15 minutes; do not allow the
water to boil hard at any
time. Check; custard should
be set and shrimp pink.

Garnish each bowl with a
lemon peel strip and a watercress sprig; put lids on and
serve immediately.

NOTE If you don't have chawan
bowls, any bowl with a lid
will do. If you don't have a
steamer, use 2 large kettles:
place 3 pyrex bowls on bottom,
top with rack and fill with
water an inch above the rack.
Be sure to wrap tea towels
around the lids so the con-
densation drops do not fall
into the soup. Everything can
be prepared ahead of time—
the surprise and delight on
the faces of your guests as
they view and taste is worth
the effort!

Other Ports of Call

I hate soup because . . .
It's often a lukewarm, nondescript mishmash;
it wilts the mustache and clouds the spectacles;
the spoon scrapes the lip and bangs the teeth
as the soup dribbles down the chin;
with trembling hand there's many a slip
twixt bowl and lip;
sipping teases, but gulping burns the mouth.
I might even be tempted to give it up
if it weren't so good

—*Anonymous*

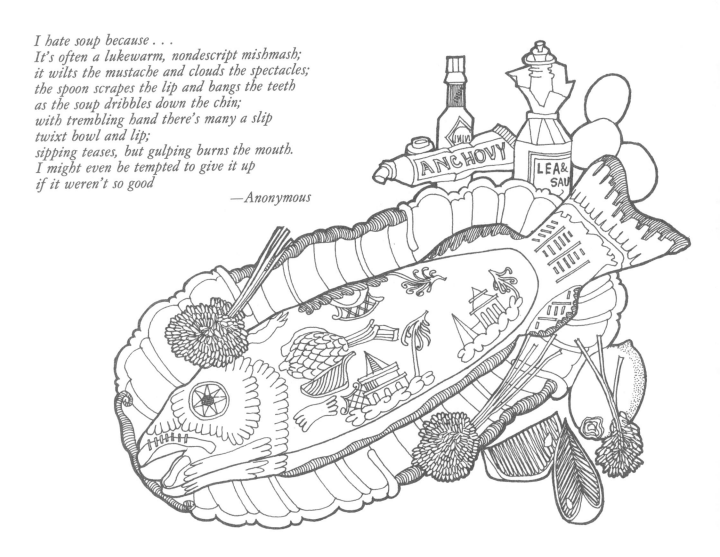

DANISH PORT SALUT SOUP

Serves 6 to 8
1 cup diced kohlrabi or
    young turnip
1/4 cup *each* minced onion
    and white part of leek
2 tablespoons butter
2 cups diced potatoes
3 cups chicken stock
2 cups milk
1/2 cup dried azuki beans,
    cooked (page 52)
1 cup heavy cream or half-
    and-half cream
2 cups shredded Danish Port
    Salut cheese
Salt and white pepper to taste
Butter, cut into bits
Minced green onions
Minced fresh parsley

Sauté kohlrabi, onion and
leek in butter until soft but
not browned. Add potatoes,
stock, milk and beans; cover,
bring to boil and simmer
gently 30 minutes. (It will
look curdled, but it doesn't
matter.)

    Add cream and 1-1/2 cups
of the cheese; cook and stir
to melt cheese and reheat; do
not boil. Season with salt and
white pepper, stir in butter
bits and serve with green
onions, parsley and remaining
cheese on top.

COCK-A-LEEKIE

Serves 6
4 cups minced leeks (white
    and some green)
2 tablespoons rendered
    chicken fat
1/2 cup hulled barley
6 cups chicken stock
6 dried prunes, pitted and
    quartered (optional)
1-1/2 cups shredded cooked
    chicken
1 cup half-and-half cream
Salt and white pepper to taste
Minced fresh parsley

Sauté leeks in chicken fat
until softened. Add barley
and stir to coat. Add stock,
cover, bring to gentle boil,
lower heat and simmer 40
minutes, or until barley is
tender. Add prunes the last
20 minutes of cooking time.

    Add chicken and cream and
reheat. Adjust seasonings with
salt and pepper and sprinkle
generously with minced parsley.

ENGLISH OXTAIL SOUP

Serves 6
1/2 cup *each* minced carrot,
    turnip and celery
3 tablespoons rendered beef
    fat and/or butter
2 tablespoons unbleached
    flour
6 to 8 cups Oxtail Stock
    (page 16)
Dry sherry to taste
Minced fresh parsley

Cook vegetables in beef fat,
covered, 5 minutes. Remove
cover and brown well. Sprinkle
with flour, cook, stirring, 3
minutes and gradually add
stock. Cook and stir until
slightly thickened. Cover, bring
to gentle boil, lower heat and
simmer 10 minutes or until
vegetables are tender. Season
to taste with sherry and sprinkle with parsley.

SOUPE A L'ADENNAISE
Belgian Cream of Endive Soup

Serves 6

1-1/4 pounds French or
  Belgium endive, sliced into
  thin rounds
1/4 cup minced leek (white
  only)
2 tablespoons minced shallots
3 tablespoons butter, for
  sautéing
2 white potatoes, scrubbed
  and cubed
2 cups brown chicken stock
1 teaspoon mixed crumbled
  dried herbs
1/2 teaspoon freshly grated
  lemon peel
1/4 teaspoon white pepper
2 cups milk
2 cups half-and-half cream
Salt
3 tablespoons butter, cut into
  bits
Paprika
Minced fresh parsley
Herb croutons

Sauté endive, leek and shallots
in butter 3 minutes, stirring
to coat. Cover and cook over
low heat 10 minutes.

Add potatoes, stock, seasonings and milk; cover, bring to
gentle boil, lower heat and
simmer 10 minutes or until
potatoes are tender-crisp.

Add cream, reheat, adjust
seasonings with salt, and swirl
in butter bits.

Sprinkle with paprika and
parsley and serve with herb
croutons.

SOUPE DE VEAU
AUX HERBES
Dutch Veal Soup with Herbs

Serves 4 to 6

3 tablespoons butter and/or
  rendered chicken fat
3 tablespoons unbleached
  flour
7 cups brown veal stock
1 tablespoon finely minced
  mixed fresh herbs, such as
  parsley, chives, savory,
  tarragon, oregano,
  marjoram
Fresh lemon juice, salt and
  white pepper to taste

1 recipe Potato Dumplings
  (following)
Minced fresh parsley
Paprika

Melt butter until bubbly, stir
in flour and cook, stirring, 3
minutes. Gradually add stock
and cook and stir until slightly
thickened. Add herbs, cover
and cook at low boil 5 minutes. Add lemon juice, salt
and pepper. Add dumplings
and garnish with parsley and
paprika.

POTATO DUMPLINGS

1 recipe Potato Dumplings
  (page 169)
3 to 4 tablespoons ground
  cooked veal
Additional 1 tablespoon
  minced fresh parsley

Make the dumplings, adding
before the additional flour
the ground veal and additional parsley. Adjust seasonings
and cook as directed.

GRAUPENSUPPE MIT HUBNERKLEIN
German Barley Soup with Giblets

Serves 4 to 6

1-1/2 to 2 pounds chicken hearts and gizzards
1 small frying chicken
8 cups chicken stock
1/4 teaspoon salt
1/8 teaspoon black pepper
Bouquet garni of
   1 large whole onion, unpeeled and stuck with 2 whole cloves
   1 rib celery, coarsely chopped
   2 large sprigs parsley
   1 bay leaf
1/2 cup hulled barley
2 tablespoons rendered chicken fat and/or butter
2 tablespoons unbleached flour
2 carrots, thinly sliced
1 small rib celery, thinly sliced
4 to 6 tender young kohlrabi, sliced
Minced fresh parsley and chives
Paprika

Trim fat from hearts and gizzards and slice. Set hearts aside and combine gizzards with chicken, stock, seasonings and bouquet garni. Cover, bring to gentle boil, lower heat and simmer 45 minutes or until chicken is tender. Remove chicken and set aside to cool. Discard bouquet garni.

Lightly brown barley in chicken fat, sprinkle with flour and cook, stirring, 3 minutes. Gradually stir in stock, cover, bring to gentle boil, lower heat and simmer 40 minutes. Add carrots and reserved hearts and continue cooking 25 minutes, adding celery and kohlrabi last 10 minutes. While soup is simmering, remove chicken meat from bones and cut into julienne pieces. Add last 5 minutes of cooking. Sprinkle with parsley and paprika.

To render meat or chicken fat, mince and melt over medium heat.

MANDELSUPPE
German Almond Soup

Serves 4

1 tablespoon minced onion
2 tablespoons butter
2 tablespoons unbleached flour
2 cups chicken stock
1 cup evaporated milk
3/4 cup blanched whole almonds, ground
1/2 teaspoon salt
1/8 teaspoon white pepper
Almond extract or rose water

Sauté onion in butter until slightly softened. Sprinkle with flour, cook, stirring, 3 minutes and gradually add stock. Cook and stir until smooth and slightly thickened. Add milk and almonds; cover and simmer 30 minutes.

Adjust seasonings to taste with salt, pepper and almond extract (be careful!).

NOTE The consistency of this soup is gritty; if smoothness is preferred, simmer the ground almonds in 1 cup stock, covered, for several hours to extract flavor. Force through sieve and add to rest of soup.

BUSECCA
Swiss Tripe Soup

Serves 6 to 8
3/4 pound honeycomb tripe
Salt, for rubbing on tripe
1 medium onion, thinly sliced
1 medium carrot, thinly sliced
1 leek, thinly sliced (white
    and some green)
1 rib celery, thinly sliced
1/2 cup chopped celery leaves
3 garlic cloves, minced
1/2 cup chopped fresh parsley
1 tablespoon chopped fresh
    oregano
2 tablespoons olive oil
8 cups brown chicken stock,
    or as needed
1 cup dried small white beans
    (navy or pea), soaked
    overnight in 2 cups water
Salt and black pepper to taste
3 large ripe tomatoes, peeled
    and quartered
3 cups shredded cabbage
1-1/2 cups shredded spinach
    or Swiss chard (optional)
Minced fresh chives
Minced garlic or freshly
    grated Parmesan cheese

Rub tripe with salt, rinse and cut into strips 1 inch long and 1/2 inch wide. Bring a kettle of salted water to boil, add tripe, cover, lower heat and cook at gentle boil 15 minutes. Drain and set tripe aside.

Cook onion, carrot, leek, celery and celery leaves, garlic and herbs in oil, covered, 10 minutes. Add stock, beans and their liquid and salt and pepper. Bring to boil, lower heat and boil gently, with lid slightly tilted, 20 minutes. Add tripe and continue cooking 35 minutes, adding tomatoes last 10 minutes and cabbage and spinach last 2 minutes. Adjust seasonings and sprinkle with chives and garlic.

VARIATIONS Add 15 minutes before end of cooking time, 2 baking potatoes, diced. Or add cooked pasta, such as orzo, with the cabbage.

A touch of garlic flavor? Steep a few lightly mashed garlic cloves in olive or safflower oil. If not using within 3 days, discard garlic.

CHLODNIK
Polish Beet Soup

Serves 3 or 4
1 garlic clove
1/4 teaspoon salt
2 to 3 cucumbers, peeled,
    seeded and finely diced
    (2 cups)
2 cups minced cooked beets
1/4 cup finely minced celery
1 cup half-and-half cream
    or milk
3-1/2 cups sour cream
3 tablespoons minced fresh
    parsley
2 tablespoons minced fresh
    chives
Salt and black pepper to taste
Julienne of beet and cucumber
Sliced radishes

Mince garlic and crush with salt; combine with cucumbers, beets and celery. Beat together half-and-half cream and sour cream and combine with parsley, chives, and cucumber-beet mixture. Add salt and pepper, chill and adjust seasonings to taste.

Serve with garnish of beet and cucumber julienne and radish slices.

KULAJDA
Czech Mushroom Soup

Serves 4 to 6

3/4 pound mushrooms, thinly
 sliced
2 tablespoons *each* butter and
 olive oil
1/4 teaspoon *each* garlic
 powder, white pepper, salt
 and crumbled dried oregano
Dash cayenne pepper
1 teaspoon caraway seeds
 (optional)
2 teaspoons fresh lemon juice
1-1/2 tablespoons unbleached
 flour
1 teaspoon paprika
3 tablespoons minced fresh
 parsley
5 cups stock of choice
1 cup sour cream
2 or 3 egg yolks
Minced fresh dill or caraway
 seeds
Paprika

Sauté mushrooms in butter
and oil, seasoning while they
are cooking with garlic powder, white pepper, salt, oregano, cayenne pepper, caraway
seeds and lemon juice, until
mushrooms are golden.

Sprinkle with flour and paprika and cook, stirring, 3
minutes. Add parsley and gradually add stock. Cook and stir
until slightly thickened. Cover
and simmer 15 minutes. Beat
together sour cream and egg
yolks, whisk in 1/2 cup hot
soup and return to rest of
soup. Reheat without boiling
and adjust seasonings to taste.

Sprinkle with dill or more
caraway seeds (if used) and
paprika. Serve with buttered
pumpernickel squares topped
with slices of Monterey Jack
or other mild cheese.

CZECH CABBAGE SOUP

Serves 4
4 cups chicken stock
2 cups shredded cabbage
1 teaspoon caraway seeds
1-1/2 teaspoons dried onion
  flakes
1 cup milk and/or half-and-
  half cream
Salt, black pepper and
  caraway seeds to taste
1/4 pound thin noodles,
  cooked al dente

Combine stock, cabbage, caraway seeds and onion, cover,
bring to boil, lower heat and
simmer until cabbage is soft.

Purée, reheat with milk and
season with salt and pepper
and more caraway seeds. Add
noodles, reheat and serve.

---

*Do not boil soups after add-
ing cream or sour cream!*

BOGRACS GULYAS
Hungarian Goulash

More than a thousand years
ago, Magyar shepherds car-
ried supplies of cooked dried
meat cubes to turn their boiling pots of selected vegetables into delicious goulash
soup. Hungarian goulash
through the years has gained
fame as a stew as well as a
soup, but who can say where
the border between them lies?

Serves 6
4 slices bacon, diced
1 cup minced onions
1 pound lean beef, cut into
  small cubes
1/2 teaspoon crumbled dried
  marjoram
1-1/2 teaspoons Hungarian
  paprika
1/2 teaspoon salt
1 teaspoon caraway seeds
1/4 teaspoon black pepper
1 garlic clove, finely minced
6 cups rich beef stock
2 ripe tomatoes, peeled and
  chopped
2 cups diced cooked potatoes
Hungarian paprika

Sauté bacon and onions until
onions are golden, stirring
often. Push to side of pan.

Raise heat, add meat; cook
and stir to brown, adding
more bacon fat if needed.
Sprinkle with seasonings and
garlic and cook and stir 3
minutes. Add stock, mix, cover and bring to boil. Lower
heat and simmer 40 minutes
or until meat is tender.

Add tomatoes and potatoes,
heat, adjust seasonings to taste
and serve with an extra sprinkling of paprika.

VARIATIONS Add cubed, cooked
carrots, celery and/or bell
pepper with the potatoes.

BORSCHT

Borscht—borsch—borsht—
borshcht. More varied by far
in its forms than in its spell-
ings. Older recipes—and some
new—call for parsley root,
which seems to be unavail-
able in most every market.

RUSSIAN TOMATO BORSHCH

Serves 3 or 4
1 cup chopped onions
2 tablespoons butter
1-1/2 cups tomato juice
1-1/2 cups dark beef stock
1/2 teaspoon *each* sour salt*
  and sugar
1 small head cabbage, finely
  shredded
1/2 cup shredded cooked
  meat, preferably from
  stock bones
Black pepper
Whipped sour cream
*See glossary

Sauté onions in butter until
soft and slightly browned.
Add tomato juice, stock, sour
salt and sugar. Cover, bring
to boil, lower heat and simmer
30 minutes. Strain.

Bring back to boil, add
cabbage and cook until tender-
crisp. Reheat with meat and
adjust seasonings to taste with
sour salt and sugar.

Sprinkle with pepper and
pass a bowl of whipped sour
cream.

EASY RUSSIAN BORSHCH

Serves 6
1-1/2 pounds beef brisket or
  meaty, lean short ribs
1 cup chopped onions
1 bay leaf
1 teaspoon salt
6 black peppercorns, lightly
  crushed
6 cups water
3 cups coarsely grated raw
  beets
1 cup coarsely grated raw
  carrots
1 cup diced potato
1 cup tomato purée
3 cups thinly shredded
  cabbage
Salt and black pepper
  to taste
Minced fresh parsley
Whipped sour cream

Combine beef, onions, bay
leaf, salt, peppercorns and
water. Cover, bring to boil,
lower heat and simmer 3
hours. Strain, cool and chill
to remove fat.

Bring stock to boil, add
beets, carrots, potato and
tomato purée. Cook 10 minutes. Add cabbage, bring back
to boil and cook until tender-
crisp. Adjust seasonings with
salt and pepper and serve
sprinkled with parsley. Pass a
bowl of whipped sour cream.

COLD RUSSIAN BORSHCH

Serves 6
2 cups tomato juice
3 green onions and tops,
  minced, crushed with 1/2
  teaspoon salt and 2 tablespoons sour cream
2 cups slivered cooked beets
1 cucumber, peeled, seeded
  and slivered
2 hard-cooked eggs, sliced
6 radishes, thinly sliced
Salt and black pepper to taste
Minced fresh dill
Whipped sour cream

Blend 1/2 cup tomato juice
with the green onion-salt-sour
cream mixture and combine
with rest of ingredients. Chill
and adjust seasonings with
salt and pepper.
  Serve in chilled bowls with
a generous sprinkling of dill
and pass a bowl of whipped
sour cream.

COLD CLEAR BORSCHT

Serves 2 or 3
1-1/2 cups grated raw beets
3 tablespoons grated onion
  and its juice
1 teaspoon *each* sour salt*
  and sugar
1 egg, well beaten
Salt and black pepper to taste
Whipped sour cream
Minced fresh chives
*See glossary

Combine beets, onion, water
to cover (2-1/2 to 3 cups),
sour salt and sugar. Cover,
bring to boil, lower heat and
simmer 30 minutes.
  Whisk 1/2 cup hot soup
into egg and return to rest of
soup. Cook and stir 3 minutes.
Do not boil.
  Strain, chill and adjust seasonings with salt and pepper.
Serve in chilled bowls garnished
with dollops of whipped sour
cream and chives.

CRIMEAN BORSHCH

Serves 10
1/4 cup minced fresh parsley
1 carrot, chopped
1 onion, chopped
2 leeks, chopped (white only)
1/2 pound lean salt pork, diced
3 tablespoons butter and/or rendered beef fat
1-1/2 pounds beef brisket or meaty, lean short ribs, cut up
8 cups water
6 black peppercorns, lightly crushed
1 bay leaf
1 teaspoon salt

8 beets, shredded
1 carrot, shredded
2 potatoes, diced
1/2 cup shredded rutabaga and/or white turnips
3 cups finely shredded cabbage
1 teaspoon *each* sour salt* and sugar
1/4 teaspoon black pepper
Minced fresh dill
Whipped sour cream
*See glossary

Sauté parsley, vegetables and salt pork in butter until golden. Add meat, water, peppercorns, bay leaf and salt. Cover, bring to boil, lower heat and simmer 2 hours. Strain, reserve and dice meat; set aside. Chill stock and remove fat.

Bring stock to boil, add 6 of the shredded beets, carrot, potatoes and rutabaga. Simmer 10 minutes. Add cabbage and reserved meat, bring to boil and cook 5 minutes. Add sour salt, sugar and pepper. Adjust to taste.

Wrap remaining 2 shredded beets in cheesecloth and squeeze out as much juice as possible. Add juice only to soup for color.

Reheat and serve sprinkled with generous amounts of dill. Pass a bowl of whipped sour cream.

VARIATION Add 1 cup tomato purée with sour salt, sugar and pepper.

RUSSIAN CABBAGE SOUP

Serves 4 to 6
1/2 pound *each* lean beef and pork butt, cubed
1/4 pound salt pork, diced
1 small cabbage, finely shredded
2 large ripe tomatoes, peeled and diced
1 cup diced onion
1 bay leaf
1/4 teaspoon black pepper
1/2 teaspoon salt
6 cups beef stock made with short ribs and marrow bones
Freshly grated Parmesan cheese or crisp bacon bits and whipped sour cream

Sauté beef, pork and salt pork to brown slightly. Add half the cabbage and all remaining ingredients, except cheese garnish. Cover, bring to boil, lower heat and simmer 1-1/2 hours, or until meat is tender. Remove bay leaf.

Bring to boil, add rest of cabbage and cook until tender-crisp.

Serve with Parmesan cheese, or sprinkle with bacon bits and pass whipped sour cream.

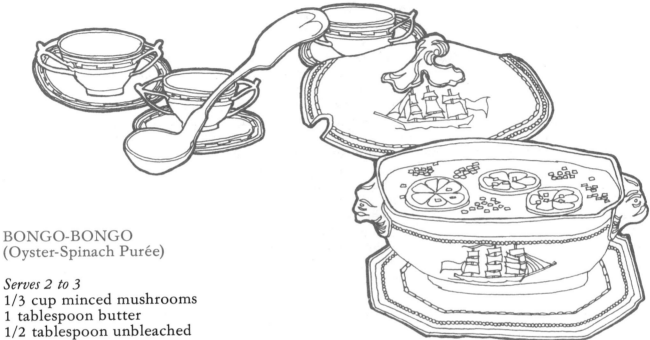

BONGO-BONGO
(Oyster-Spinach Purée)

Serves 2 to 3

1/3 cup minced mushrooms
1 tablespoon butter
1/2 tablespoon unbleached
   flour
1 cup milk
8 ounces shucked oysters and
   liquor
1/2 cup well-drained and
   chopped cooked spinach
1-1/2 cups half-and-half cream
1/4 teaspoon garlic powder
1 teaspoon Worcestershire
   sauce
1/4 teaspoon ground thyme
Salt and black pepper to taste
Lemon slices

Sauté mushrooms in butter until soft, sprinkle with flour and cook, stirring, 3 minutes. Gradually add milk; cook and stir until smooth and slightly thickened. Purée with oysters and liquor and spinach. Reheat with cream and seasonings; adjust to taste. Cool, chill and serve in chilled bowls garnished with lemon slices.

VARIATION To serve hot, heat with 2 tablespoons butter and garnish with lemon slices and dollops of sour cream whipped with a little soy sauce.

MIDEAST BARLEY-LENTIL SOUP

Serves 6

1 large onion, sliced into rings
1 or 2 garlic cloves, finely minced
2 cups finely shredded spinach
4 tablespoons butter and/or rendered chicken fat
1/3 cup hulled barley
6 to 8 cups lamb or chicken stock
1 cup dried brown lentils
1 cup minced fresh parsley
2 ripe tomatoes, peeled and diced

Cook onion, garlic and spinach in butter, covered, 5 minutes. Remove with slotted spoon and set aside. Lightly brown barley in same pot and add stock. Cover, bring to gentle boil, lower heat and simmer 30 minutes. Add lentils and parsley and continue simmering 30 minutes, adding reserved onion mixture last 5 minutes. Stir in tomatoes.

PEANUT SOUP

Serves 4 to 6

2 teaspoons grated onion
1/2 cup unsalted raw peanuts, ground
3 tablespoons butter
2 tablespoons unbleached flour
3-1/2 cups brown chicken stock
1 egg yolk, beaten
1 cup heavy cream
Minced fresh chili pepper, celery salt, white pepper and fresh lemon juice to taste
Lemon slices
Toasted peanuts

Sauté onion and peanuts in butter 5 minutes, stirring constantly. Sprinkle with flour, cook, stirring, 3 minutes, and gradually add stock. Cook and stir until smooth and slightly thickened; cover and simmer gently 15 to 20 minutes.

Beat together yolk and cream, whisk in 1/2 cup hot soup, and return to rest of soup. Season with chili pepper, celery salt, white pepper and lemon juice; thin with more stock if desired. Reheat, but do not boil.

Serve with lemon slices and toasted peanuts.

VARIATION Add 2 tablespoons *each* finely minced red and green bell pepper the last few minutes of cooking.

PEANUT BUTTER SOUP

Serves 4 to 6

2 tablespoons butter
2 tablespoons unbleached flour
4 cups milk
3/4 cup chopped onion
2 tablespoons freshly grated Parmesan cheese
1/4 teaspoon celery seed
1/2 teaspoon salt
1/4 teaspoon black pepper
1 bay leaf, crumbled
1/3 cup smooth peanut butter
Crisp bacon bits or chopped roasted peanuts

Melt butter until bubbly, sprinkle with flour and cook, stirring, 3 minutes. Gradually add milk; cook and stir until smooth and slightly thickened.

Add onion, cheese, seasonings, bay leaf and peanut butter. Cover, bring to boil and simmer 15 minutes. Strain and adjust seasonings. Garnish with bacon bits.

A Meal in a Bowl

Drink's bad effects may in a great
measure be taken off by a dinner
of mutton broth, or soup maigre,
on the following day.
—A. Hunter, "Culina," 1806

Boisterous, medieval knights clutching dripping chunks of meat from a giant bowl may come to mind when thinking of soup as a complete meal. Generally these hearty soups contain chunks of solid food and therefore should be served in broad, shallow bowls with knives and forks, as well as spoons.

Sour French bread and unsalted butter make ideal accompaniments. Small salads and light desserts go well with these soups, too.

SEAFOOD GUMBO

Serves 8 to 10

One 2-pound chicken, cut up
2 tablespoons butter and/or rendered chicken fat
10 cups chicken stock
1 teaspoon paprika
2 garlic cloves
1/2 cup celery leaves, chopped
1/2 teaspoon ground turmeric

1/4 pound lean ham, cubed
1/2 cup diced celery
1 bunch green onions and tops, chopped
1 leek, chopped (white and some green)
2 tablespoons butter and/or rendered chicken fat
2 tablespoons unbleached flour
1 teaspoon paprika
1/2 teaspoon black pepper
Bouquet garni of
    8 sprigs parsley
    1 sprig thyme
    1 bay leaf
    4 cloves
    4 allspice berries, lightly crushed
1/4 pound crab legs
1/4 pound canned or bay shrimp
1-1/2 pints shucked oysters, frizzled in butter and own juices 3 minutes
Salt, black pepper, Worcestershire sauce and Tabasco sauce to taste
1 teaspoon filé powder*
Minced fresh parsley
Paprika
*See glossary

Brown chicken in butter; add stock, paprika, garlic, celery leaves and turmeric. Cover, bring to boil, lower heat and simmer gently 1 hour, or until chicken is tender. Cool and remove chicken from bones, cut up and reserve. Strain stock.

Brown ham, celery, green onions and leek in butter. Sprinkle with flour, cook, stirring, 3 minutes, and deglaze with 2 cups of the reserved stock, scraping the bottom of pan. Add rest of stock, paprika, pepper, and bouquet garni. Cover and simmer 1 hour.

Discard bouquet garni. Add crab, shrimp, oysters and reserved chicken. Reheat carefully and adjust seasonings with salt, pepper, Worcestershire sauce and Tabasco.

Remove from heat, stir in filé, and sprinkle with minced parsley and paprika. Serve with garlic French bread.

VARIATION Add 2 cups stewed tomatoes or 1/4 cup tomato paste. Serve with bowls of fluffy white rice.

Omit filé powder. Add 1 cup cut-up cooked okra with crab.

BOUILLABAISSE

Immortalized in Thackery's ballad as "a noble dish—a sort of soup, or broth, or brew," a bouillabaisse is a general category more than a particular soup.

Serves 10 to 12
3/4 cup minced onion
1/4 cup minced white of leek
6 garlic cloves, minced
1 sprig fennel
3 sprigs parsley, crushed
1 bay leaf
Peel from 1/2 orange
5 to 6 pounds of fresh sea-
    food, some from each of the
    following categories:

CRUSTACEANS:
crab, shrimp, crayfish,
    langoustes, lobster

FIRM:
sea bass, flounder, grunt,
    haddock, perch, scrod, red
    snapper, gray snapper, sea
    trout, rockfish, halibut

DELICATE:
whiting, red mullet,
    sablefish, sole

1/2 to 3/4 cup olive oil
1/2 teaspoon salt
1/4 teaspoon black pepper
Pinch saffron threads
12 cups fish stock, or 8
    cups fish stock and 4 cups
    dry white wine
10 to 12 stale French bread
    slices
Aioli Sauce (page 172,
    optional)

Put vegetables, herbs and orange peel in large kettle. Arrange selected cleaned crustaceans over vegetables and top with firm fish of choice. Pour olive oil over and sprinkle with salt, pepper and saffron. Add liquid, cover and bring to fast boil; quick cooking is essential to the consistency. Boil 7 minutes, add delicate fish of choice and cook 6 more minutes. Do not cook more than 15 minutes in all. Place a slice of bread in each bowl. Arrange crustaceans and fish on a platter to be served separately. Adjust flavor of broth and moisten each piece of bread. Serve rest of broth in tureen. Serve with Aioli Sauce.

VARIATION Quartered or sliced potatoes may be added at the same time as the firm fish.

BOURRIDE
Basque-Style Fish Soup

Serves 8
8 cups water
1-1/2 cups chopped onions
2 tomatoes, chopped
3 sprigs parsley
1 sprig oregano
1 bay leaf
6 coriander seeds
1 cup chopped celery
3 garlic cloves
Peel from 1/2 orange
1 teaspoon salt
4 black peppercorns, lightly
    crushed
Pinch saffron threads
2 tablespoons olive oil
2 pounds fish fillets, such as
    flounder, bass, red snapper,
    butter fish (4 fillets)
8 slices stale French bread
Salt and black pepper to taste
2 egg yolks, beaten
Aioli Sauce (page 172)

Bring water, vegetables, herbs, seasonings and oil to boil, cover, lower heat and simmer 20 minutes. Wrap fish in cheesecloth, raise heat, add fish, lower heat and poach gently 10 to 12 minutes until just tender.

Place a slice of bread into each of 8 bowls, top with half a fillet, and keep warm.

Strain stock and adjust seasonings with salt and pepper. Whisk 1/2 cup hot soup into egg yolks and return to rest of soup. Ladle soup into bowls and top each serving with 1 tablespoon Aioli Sauce.

OYSTER STEW

Making oyster stew is a matter of personal taste. Choose your own seasonings from those I've suggested.

Serves 4
1 small rib celery, thinly
    sliced on diagonal
1 tablespoon minced onion
1/2 teaspoon pressed garlic
2 tablespoons butter
1-1/2 pints shucked oysters
3 cups half-and-half cream
1 cup clam juice
Suggested seasonings: Wor-
    cestershire sauce, black
    pepper, cayenne pepper,
    ground thyme, minced
    fresh tarragon, fresh
    lemon juice and salt
Butter, cut into bits
Chopped fresh celery leaves
    or parsley

Cook celery, onion and garlic in butter, covered, until celery is tender-crisp.

Combine oyster liquor with cream and clam juice and seasonings of choice. Bring just to boil and add oysters and celery-onion-garlic mixture. Bring back to boil and cook only long enough to curl the edges of the oysters. Do not overcook. Swirl in butter bits.

Garnish with celery leaves.

TURKEY WITH OYSTERS

Serves 6

4 ribs celery, sliced on
diagonal
1/2 cup *each* diced onion and
leeks
1 garlic clove, minced
4 tablespoons butter and/or
rendered chicken fat
5 tablespoons unbleached
flour
2 cups milk or half-and-half
cream
4 cups turkey broth
2 cups diced cooked turkey
1/2 teaspoon *each* freshly
grated nutmeg, white
pepper and salt
1 teaspoon fresh lemon juice
1 pint shucked oysters,
frizzled in 1 tablespoon
butter
Minced fresh parsley

Sauté celery, onion, leeks and
garlic in butter until onion
is soft. Sprinkle with flour,
cook, stirring, 3 minutes, and
gradually add milk and broth.
Cook and stir until smooth
and thickened.

Add turkey, reheat and season with nutmeg, pepper, salt
and lemon juice. Adjust to
taste.

Add oysters to hot soup
and serve immediately with a
generous sprinkling of minced
parsley.

VARIATION Garnish with finely
minced raw celery and leaves.

EAST INDIAN MULLIGATAWNEY

Serves 6

One 2-1/2- to 3-pound chicken,
cut up
1 teaspoon paprika
1/2 teaspoon salt
1/4 teaspoon black pepper
3 to 4 tablespoons rendered
chicken fat
1/3 cup *each* diced turnip,
carrot, onion, celery, and
peeled tart apple
1 tablespoon rice flour
1 to 2 teaspoons curry powder
6 cups chicken stock
Bouquet garni of
    1 bay leaf
    3 sprigs parsley
    1 sprig thyme
    6 black peppercorns,
    lightly crushed
    2 whole cloves
1/4 cup minced bell pepper
1/8 teaspoon ground mace
1/4 teaspoon black pepper
1/2 teaspoon salt
1/4 to 1/2 cup tomato sauce
(optional)
1/4 teaspoon sugar (optional)
1 recipe Lemon Rice Balls
(following)

Sprinkle chicken with pa-
prika, salt and pepper and
sauté a few pieces at a time in
fat. Remove and set aside.
Add vegetables and apple to
pan; stir and cook until golden.

Sprinkle with flour and curry powder, cook, stirring, 3
minutes, gradually add stock,
and cook and stir until smooth.
Add chicken, bouquet garni,
bell pepper and seasonings.
Cover, bring to boil and simmer until chicken is tender.
Remove chicken and cut meat
into small pieces. Set aside.

Strain broth, forcing as
much pulp through sieve as
possible. Heat, adjust seasonings and add tomato sauce
and sugar.

Serve with Lemon Rice Balls
and as much chicken as desired.

VARIATION Add puréed cooked
garbanzo beans with tomato
sauce and combine thoroughly.

LEMON RICE BALLS

3/4 cup raw long-grain white
   rice, well washed
1-1/2 cups plus 2 tablespoons
   water
1-1/2 tablespoons fresh
   lemon juice
1/2 teaspoon freshly grated
   lemon peel
1/2 teaspoon salt
1/4 teaspoon black pepper
2 to 3 tablespoons garlic
   olive oil

Spread rice evenly on the bottom of a saucepan; combine water and lemon juice and add to rice. Let stand at least 1 hour. Bring to boil over high heat, uncovered, and reduce heat slightly. Cook until all the water has evaporated from surface. Cover immediately and cook at lowest heat 30 to 40 minutes. Rice should be sticky but not gooey.

Season with lemon peel, salt and pepper, stirring in with a fork. Adjust seasonings to taste.

When cool enough to handle, form rice into 30 marble-sized balls. (If it cools off too much, you may need to dip your fingers in water.) These may be made ahead and kept at room temperature up to 4 hours. Sauté balls in oil, turning several times, until they barely start to turn golden. Do not sauté too long or they will become crusty. Drain on paper toweling and serve immediately.

CREAM OF CHICKEN WITH VEGETABLES

Serves 6 to 8

One 2-1/2- to 3-pound chicken
2 cups beef stock
4 cups chicken stock
1 whole onion stuck with
  3 cloves
1 leek, chopped (white and
  some green)
1 carrot, chopped
1 cup chopped celery
3 green onions and tops,
  chopped
1 sprig *each* marjoram and
  thyme
3 sprigs parsley
1 teaspoon salt
6 black peppercorns, lightly
  crushed
3 egg yolks, beaten
1 cup heavy cream
1 cup chopped cooked vegetables, such as mushrooms,
  cauliflower, broccoli, green
  beans, peas, corn
1/2 to 1 cup half-and-half
  cream
1/2 teaspoon salt
1/4 teaspoon white pepper
1 tablespoon fresh lemon
  juice
1/4 to 1/2 teaspoon minced
  fresh tarragon
Freshly grated Cheddar
  cheese or raw carrot

Combine chicken, stocks, vegetables, herbs, salt and peppercorns. Cover, bring to boil,
lower heat and simmer 1
hour, or until chicken is tender. Remove chicken and cool;
strain broth, cool and chill to
remove fat.

Remove meat from chicken,
julienne 2 cups of white meat
and reserve. Dice 1-1/2 cups
dark meat and purée with 1
cup of broth. Return to rest
of broth and reheat.

Beat together yolks and
heavy cream, whisk in 1/2
cup hot soup and return to
rest of soup. Add vegetables
and white chicken meat. Reheat, but do not boil.

Thin with half-and-half cream
and season with salt, pepper,
lemon juice and tarragon. Adjust seasonings and serve with
a garnish of grated Cheddar
cheese.

Be sure to stir well when
serving, as puréed dark meat
tends to settle on the bottom.

SPLIT PEA SOUP

Serves 6 to 8

3 or 4 ham hocks and/or
  bones with meat
1 pair pig's feet, blanched
  and rinsed
2 cups sliced onion
1 cup chopped carrots
2 garlic cloves, minced
2 cups chopped celery and
  leaves
2 tablespoons butter and/or
  rendered ham fat
1-1/2 cups dried green and/or
  yellow split peas
12 black peppercorns, lightly
  crushed
3 sprigs parsley
1 bay leaf
2 tablespoons crumbled dried
  fines herbes
6 cups water and juice from
  canned ham and/or chicken
  stock
1 cup evaporated milk
Additional water or stock,
  if needed
Crumbled dried marjoram,
  salt and black pepper to
  taste
Dry sherry

Brown ham hocks and/or bones, pig's feet and vegetables in butter.

Add peas, peppercorns, herbs and water, juice and/or stock. Cover, bring to boil, lower heat and simmer, stirring occasionally, 3 hours. Remove ham hock and pig's feet. Dice meat and set aside.

Force through food mill or sieve, pushing as much pulp through as possible. Reheat with reserved meat and evaporated milk, thin with stock if desired, and adjust seasonings with marjoram, salt and pepper.

Just before serving add dry sherry to taste.

VARIATION For a heartier meal, add cooked sausages, browned mushrooms, diced potato and/or vegetable julienne. Sprinkle with freshly grated Parmesan cheese.

BRAZILIAN BEAN SOUP

Serves 6 to 8
2 cups dried Latin American black beans*
8 cups hot water
1 teaspoon salt
1 cup tomato sauce
1 large onion, minced
1 large garlic clove, minced
2 ounces salt pork, diced
2 or more small dried red chili peppers
3/4 pound fresh pork, cubed
1/2 pound Portuguese linguesa sausage
1/4 teaspoon black pepper
Orange slices
Watercress sprigs
*See glossary

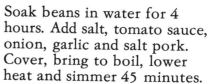

Soak beans in water for 4 hours. Add salt, tomato sauce, onion, garlic and salt pork. Cover, bring to boil, lower heat and simmer 45 minutes.

Add chili peppers, pork, sausage and black pepper. Bring back to boil, lower heat and simmer until beans are cooked but still hold their shape. Discard chili peppers. Adjust seasonings to taste. Pass iced orange slices and watercress sprigs. Serve with hot French rolls.

NOTE If you prefer a less spicy soup, use only a small amount of chili pepper.

VARIATION Serve with cooked kale or collard greens and plain rice.

SCOTCH BROTH

This is a simple, rather bland soup. Serve with a tangy salad and hard rolls.

Serves 6 to 8
4 cups lamb or veal stock
Leftover lamb and bones
2 cups water
3/4 cup pearl barley
1/2 cup diced turnip
3/4 cup diced carrots
1/2 cup diced leeks (white and some green)
1 cup diced celery
1 cup diced mushrooms
3 tomatoes, peeled and diced
Salt and black pepper to taste

Combine stock, leftover lamb and bones, water and barley. Cover, bring to boil, lower heat and simmer 1/2 hour.

Remove meat and bones, shred meat and set aside. Continue cooking soup 1 hour or until barley is softened.

Add turnip, carrots, leeks and celery; cook 15 minutes. Add mushrooms and tomatoes and cook 5 more minutes. Add shredded lamb and reheat. Adjust seasonings with salt and pepper. Soup should be thick.

LAMB WITH MINT

A rich luncheon or supper soup to be served in small portions.

Serves 5 or 6
3-1/2 to 4 pounds meaty
    lamb blocks
1 cup dry red wine
6 cups water
1 whole onion stuck with 3
    cloves
Bouquet garni of
    4 sprigs parsley
    2 sprigs savory
    1 sprig thyme
    1 bay leaf
    6 black peppercorns,
        lightly crushed
2 ribs celery and leaves,
    chopped
3 parsnips, diced
2 teaspoons salt
1/2 cup diced celery root
2 cups shelled green peas
2 tablespoons minced leek
    (white and some green)
Salt and black pepper to taste
1/2 cup minced fresh mint

Combine lamb blocks, wine, water, onion, bouquet garni, celery, parsnips and salt. Cover, bring to boil, lower heat and simmer 3 hours until lamb is tender. Remove lamb, sliver meat to make 1-1/2 cups and set aside. Strain stock, cool and chill to remove fat.

Bring back to boil with celery root, peas and leek, cover and simmer 15 minutes or until vegetables are soft. Purée.

Add slivered lamb, reheat and adjust seasonings with salt and pepper.

Sprinkle with mint, bring *just* to boil and serve immediately.

No fresh herbs in your garden? Use one-third to one-half the amount dried.

LAMB WITH MILLET

Serves 4 to 6
1 recipe stock from Lamb
    with Mint (preceding)
1 cup millet
2/3 cup *each* lima beans and
    sliced carrot, celery and
    onion
2 tablespoons butter and/or
    corn oil
2 to 3 cups shredded beet
    greens, spinach or Swiss
    chard
Salt, black pepper and fresh
    lime juice to taste

Prepare the stock as directed, reserving the meat from the lamb blocks. Brown the millet and vegetables in butter, stirring to coat well. Add stock, cover, bring to boil, lower heat and cook at gentle boil 30 minutes, or until millet is tender. Stir in beet greens, bring back to boil and cook 1 to 2 minutes until greens are limp. Add reserved lamb and adjust seasonings with salt, pepper and lime juice.

THICK OXTAIL SOUP

Serves 4 to 6
2-1/2 pounds oxtails, cut up
1 cup chopped onions
3 garlic cloves, minced
2 ribs celery, chopped
1 teaspoon salt
7 cups water
1/2 cup hulled barley
1/2 cup dried lentils
Salt and black pepper to taste
Minced fresh parsley

Combine oxtails, onions, garlic, celery, salt and water; cover, bring to boil and cook 1-1/2 hours at low boil. Skim off any scum that rises to the surface.

Cool, chill and defat. Reheat, add barley and cook rapidly 30 minutes, adding water if needed as the barley swells.

Add lentils and cook another 30 minutes until barley and lentils are tender but lentils still hold their shape. Add water if the soup is too thick, reheat, adjust seasonings with salt and pepper and serve with a generous sprinkling of minced parsley.

Many soups, such as lentil and oxtail, improve with reheating, so save time by making a day ahead.

HERB OXTAIL SOUP

Serves 4 to 6
2-1/2 pounds oxtails, cut up
2 tablespoons butter and/or rendered beef fat
1/4 teaspoon *each* salt and celery salt
1/2 teaspoon white pepper
1 cup chopped onions
2 garlic cloves, minced
3 tablespoons mushroom concentrate (page 14)
3 cups dry red wine
2 cups water
Bouquet garni of
    2 sprigs parsley
    1 sprig rosemary
    1 sprig thyme
    2 sprigs oregano
1/2 cup dried lima, garbanzo, pinto, cranberry or beans of choice
1 cup sliced carrots
1 cup diced potatoes
3 cups dark beef stock
1-1/2 cups vegetable or tomato juice (optional)
1/2 cup Madeira, or to taste

Brown oxtails in butter on all sides, sprinkling with salt, celery salt and pepper as they are cooking. Add onions and garlic the last turn, brown and add mushroom concentrate, wine, water and bouquet garni. Cover, bring to boil, lower heat and simmer 1-1/2 hours. Cool, chill and remove fat.

Bring back to boil. Add beans, cover, lower heat and simmer 1-1/2 hours.

Remove bouquet garni, add carrots, potatoes, stock and juice. Bring back to boil and cook 15 minutes or until vegetables are tender-crisp. Adjust seasonings.

Just before serving, add Madeira.

CREAMY MINESTRONE WITH PESTO

Serves 6
2 tablespoons minced onion
1/2 cup minced celery
2 teaspoons olive oil
2 turnips and tops, bulbs minced and tops finely chopped
1/2 cup finely shredded cabbage
1/2 cup finely chopped beet greens or Swiss chard, stems and ribs removed
1/4 cup minced fresh parsley
1/2 teaspoon salt
1/4 teaspoon black pepper
5 cups brown veal or chicken stock
2 cups half-and-half cream
Salt, black pepper and minced fresh oregano to taste
1 recipe Pesto (following)
Freshly grated Parmesan cheese

Sauté onion and celery in oil until soft. Add vegetables, parsley, salt, pepper and stock. Cover, bring to boil, lower heat and simmer 20 minutes until vegetables are tender. Add cream, reheat and adjust seasonings with salt, pepper and oregano.

Just before serving drizzle Pesto over top and pass Parmesan cheese.

PESTO

1/4 cup minced fresh basil
1 garlic clove, minced
1/2 cup freshly grated Parmesan cheese
1 tablespoon olive oil

Mash basil, garlic and cheese; add oil as needed to make a paste.

Make a double or triple recipe of Pesto. Reserve the portion not used in soup for tossing with freshly cooked pasta the next night.

MIDEAST BEAN SOUP

Serves 8 to 10
1 cup dried red kidney beans
1 cup dried garbanzo beans
4 cups water
1 large leek, sliced (white and a little green)
1 large onion, sliced
1/2 teaspoon ground turmeric
1/4 teaspoon cayenne pepper
1/4 cup olive oil
2 quarts lamb stock
3/4 cup raw long-grain brown rice
1 cup brown lentils
Salt and black pepper to taste
3 medium beets, cut in julienne
2 cups loosely packed shredded Swiss chard
1/4 cup fresh lemon juice
Minced fresh parsley
Plain yoghurt

Soak kidney and garbanzo beans in water overnight. Sauté leek, onion, turmeric and cayenne pepper in oil until translucent. Add stock and beans and their liquid, bring to gentle boil, lower heat and simmer, with lid slightly tilted, 1 hour. Add brown rice, lentils, salt and pepper, bring back to gentle boil, cover, lower heat and simmer 30 minutes, adding beets last 15 minutes and chard last 5 minutes. Stir in lemon juice, cook 2 or 3 minutes and adjust seasonings. Sprinkle with parsley and pass yoghurt.

ITALIAN BREAD AND CABBAGE SOUP

Serves 4 to 6
8 slices stale sourdough bread
3 to 5 garlic cloves, pressed
1-1/2 cups finely shredded
 cabbage
3/4 cup finely sliced onion
1 cup tomato sauce
1/2 teaspoon salt
1/4 teaspoon black pepper
3 tablespoons *each* freshly
 grated Parmesan and
 Romano cheese
6 cups dark beef stock
Minced fresh Italian parsley

Cover the bottom of a large Dutch oven or casserole (with a tight lid) with bread, overlapping the slices. Layer the garlic, cabbage and onion on top of the bread. Spread tomato sauce over top and sprinkle with salt, pepper and cheeses. *Carefully* pour in stock without disturbing the layers. Cover and bake in a 375° oven 45 minutes. Check after 30 minutes and add extra stock if the soup appears to be too thick.

Serve with a generous sprinkling of parsley.

Some Like it Cold

Let there be two great dishes of
soup meagre, a good large suet
pudding . . . and a dish of
artichokes.
—*Fielding's Miser, 1737*

Many people, disenchanted with mere flavoring, sugar, cyclamates, saccharin, malt, hops, alcohol, fizz water and other nonfoods, are discovering the pleasures of tasty cold soups.

Here you'll find soups that are best cold, along with some equally good hot or cold. Elsewhere other soups, too, suggest serving cold as an option.

Both dishes and soup should be chilled in the refrigerator all day or overnight, and chilled individual bowls or serving bowl should be nested in crushed ice if at all possible. Adjust seasonings *after chilling,* embellish with any of the garnitures that appeal, and serve with toasts, croutons or other accompaniments.

ARTICHOKE PUREE

Serves 3
1 can (10-1/2 ounce) *water-pack* artichoke hearts
2 cups slightly gelatinous chicken stock
1/4 to 1/2 teaspoon crumbled dried oregano
1/2 teaspoon chicken stock base
1/4 teaspoon salt
2 tablespoons fresh lemon juice
1/2 cup half-and-half cream
1/2 cup heavy cream
Thinly sliced lemon
Minced fresh parsley and/or chives
Sour cream whipped with soy sauce

Drain artichoke hearts and purée with stock and oregano. Pour into saucepan and heat slowly. Add seasonings and creams and adjust to taste. Cool, chill and adjust seasonings.

Serve with garnish of lemon slices, parsley and/or chives and small dollops of sour cream.

VARIATION Pass a tray of crab or bay or canned shrimp and/or julienned cooked chicken or pork, and halved cherry tomatoes.

If your chicken stock is too gelatinous for cold soups, thin with water and/or milk and flavor with chicken stock base.

AVOCADO PUREE

Serves 4 to 6
4 large ripe avocados
2 tablespoons fresh lemon
    juice
1/2 cup sour cream
1 to 2 tablespoons chicken
    stock base
3 cups half-and-half cream
1/4 teaspoon salt
1/8 teaspoon white pepper
1/4 teaspoon garlic powder
1 teaspoon grated onion
Bay or canned shrimp
Minced fresh chervil
Paprika
Freshly ground white pepper

Purée all ingredients, except shrimp, chervil, paprika and freshly ground pepper, and chill. Adjust seasonings. Serve garnished with shrimp, chervil and a sprinkling of paprika. Pass the peppermill.

VARIATION Season with white rum and/or curry powder; or sprinkle with a generous amount of minced fresh dill.

ASPARAGUS PUREE

Serves 6 to 8
2-1/2 pounds asparagus,
    trimmed and washed
3 cups peeled and chopped
    ripe tomatoes
4 to 6 basil leaves
1/4 teaspoon white pepper
6 cups chicken stock
3 tablespoons rice flour
1/2 cup sour cream
Salt
Half-and-half cream (optional)
Curried toast fingers

Cut off 20 2-inch tips of asparagus and cut rest of stalks into 1-inch pieces. Cook the asparagus and tips, tomatoes, basil and pepper in 2 cups of the stock, removing the tips when they are just tender-crisp. Reserve the tips for garnish. Continue cooking mixture 20 minutes or until stems are tender; purée.

Combine remaining stock, flour and sour cream with purée; cook and stir until smooth and slightly thickened. Force through medium-fine sieve and add salt to taste. Thin with half-and-half cream, if desired. Chill thoroughly, adjust seasoning and garnish with reserved asparagus tips. Serve with curried toast fingers.

VARIATION Garnish with cooked crab legs and/or shrimp and a generous sprinkling of minced fresh parsley and chives.

CUCUMBER MADRILENE

Serves 6
2 cups cooked shrimp
2 cucumbers, peeled, seeded and grated
3 tablespoons grated onion
2 teapoons fresh lemon juice
1/4 to 1/2 teaspoon salt
1/4 teaspoon white pepper
2 to 3 tablespoons minced fresh mint
1 recipe Jellied Madrilène (page 20)
Extra minced fresh mint

Finely dice 1 cup of the shrimp and combine with onion, lemon juice, salt, pepper, 2 to 3 tablespoons mint and madrilène. Chill until set. Serve with remaining shrimp and more minced mint.

When serving cold soups, make sure that seasonings have been adjusted after chilling and that the soup and the serving bowls are thoroughly chilled.

GREEN BEAN PUREE

Serves 4 to 6
1 pound green beans, cut up
2 cups *each* lamb and pork stock
1/2 cup sour cream
1-1/2 cups half-and-half cream
1 teaspoon fresh lemon juice
1/4 teaspoon salt
1/8 teaspoon *each* white pepper and ground savory
Lemon slices
Minced fresh parsley

Cook beans in stock until tender; purée and cool.

Beat sour cream with a little half-and-half, combine with purée and season with lemon juice, salt, pepper and savory. Add remaining cream. Chill, adjust seasonings and garnish with lemon slices and parsley.

PARSLEY VELOUTE

Serves 6
2 large bunches parsley
5 cups stock of choice
1/4 cup raw brown rice
2 tablespoons butter and/or
   rendered chicken fat
1/4 cup minced onion
Salt, celery salt and white
   and cayenne pepper to taste
2 egg yolks, lightly beaten
1-1/2 cups milk or half-and-
   half cream
1/2 cup heavy cream
Fresh lemon juice to taste
Plain yoghurt or sour cream
Peeled and chopped ripe
   tomato

Remove large stems from
parsley, chop and combine
with stock. Mince the leaves
and tender stems; set aside.
Cook stems and stock, covered,
30 minutes at low boil. Strain
and set stock aside.

Lightly brown rice in butter.
Add onion and all but 1/2
cup of the minced parsley.
Cover and cook, stirring to
coat, 5 minutes. Add stock
and seasonings, cover, bring
to gentle boil, lower heat and
simmer 45 minutes until rice
is tender. Purée and reheat.
Beat together egg yolks and
milk, whisk in 1/2 cup hot
soup and return to rest of
soup. Cool, add heavy cream
and lemon juice and chill
thoroughly. Adjust seasonings
and serve with dollops of
yoghurt, reserved parsley and
tomato.

PARSLEY-LEEK VELOUTE Substitute for the onion 1/3 cup
thinly sliced white of leek.
Garnish with minced mush-
rooms that have been sprinkled
with fresh lemon juice. Grate
a little lemon peel over.

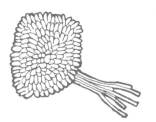

CREAMY PUMPKIN SOUP

Serves 4 to 6
1/4 cup minced onion
2 tablespoons minced leek
   (white and some green)
2 tablespoons butter
3 cups chicken stock
2 cups fresh pumpkin purée
1/2 teaspoon sugar
1/4 to 1/2 teaspoon ground
   mace
Chicken stock base, white
   pepper and salt to taste
Half-and-half cream
Whipped cream

Sauté onion and leek in
butter until soft. Add chicken
stock and pumpkin; mix well
and heat. Purée and force
through sieve.
   Add seasonings, chill thoroughly and adjust seasonings.
Thin with cream, if desired,
and serve with dollops of
whipped cream.

VARIATION Garnish with coriander sprigs.

SPINACH PUREE

Serves 4 to 6
1 pound fresh spinach,
  coarsely chopped (6 to 7
  cups loosely packed)
2 cups chicken stock
1/4 cup chopped green
  onions and tops
1/4 cup *each* minced fresh
  parsley and dill
1 teaspoon chicken stock
  base
1 cup water
Pinch sugar
1/8 teaspoon freshly grated
  nutmeg
1/4 teaspoon salt
1/8 teaspoon white pepper
1 cup heavy cream
2 tablespoons dry sherry
Cold cooked lobster or shrimp
Paprika
Lemon wedges

Boil spinach in stock 10 minutes. Purée with green onions,
parsley and dill.

Dissolve stock base in water,
blend with seasonings, spinach
mixture, cream and sherry.
Chill.

Adjust seasonings and arrange
thin slices of cold cooked
lobster around edge of bowls.
Sprinkle with paprika and
serve with lemon wedges.

VARIATION Float a teaspoon
of peeled, seeded and coarsely
grated cucumber on each serving of soup.

FRESH CORN AND ZUCCHINI SOUP

Serves 6
2 large ears corn
1/2 cup minced onion
1 teaspoon finely minced
  garlic
2 tablespoons olive oil
6 cups lamb or beef stock
4 sprigs parsley
1 sprig oregano
2 unpeeled new potatoes,
  diced
2 to 3 cups shredded zucchini
1/4 teaspoon salt
1/8 teaspoon white pepper
1 cup heavy cream
Finely chopped hard-cooked
  eggs
Minced fresh chives
Paprika

Cut kernels from corn and set
aside. Cut cobs into several
pieces and set aside. Lightly
brown onion and garlic in oil,
add stock, parsley, oregano
and cut-up cobs. Bring to
boil and cook 5 minutes.
Discard parsley, oregano and
cobs. Add reserved corn kernels and potatoes. Bring to
gentle boil, cover, lower heat
and simmer 5 minutes or
until corn and potatoes are
almost tender. Add zucchini,
salt and pepper. Bring back
to gentle boil, cover, lower
heat and cook 3 minutes or
until zucchini is cooked but
still crisp. Remove from heat
and add cream. Chill at least
4 hours, adjust seasonings
and garnish with hard-cooked
egg, chives and paprika.

*Colorful, tasty garnishes can
turn a simple soup into a
spectacular one.*

VICHYSOISSE

Serves 6 to 8
1-1/2 cups minced leeks
   (white and some green)
1/4 cup minced onion
1 garlic clove, minced
4 tablespoons butter and/or
   rendered chicken fat
3 cups brown chicken stock,
   or combination of chicken
   and beef stocks
1/2 tablespoon mushroom
   concentrate (page 14)
1/4 teaspoon white pepper
2 cups diced baking potatoes
3 cups milk
1 cup heavy cream
Salt, white pepper and fresh
   lemon juice to taste
Minced fresh dill or green
   onion tops

Cook leeks, onion and garlic in butter, covered, until soft. Add stock, seasonings and potatoes; cover, bring to boil, lower heat and simmer until potatoes are soft.

Purée, add milk and cream, blend well and chill.

Adjust seasonings with salt, pepper and lemon juice. Serve with a sprinkling of dill.

VARIATION Omit mushroom concentrate and season with ground mace or freshly grated nutmeg. Sprinkle with paprika and minced fresh chives.

A bitter cucumber can ruin a soup. Taste first!

CUCUMBER VICHYSOISSE

Serves 6 to 8
3 tablespoons minced green
   onions and tops
3 tablespoons minced onion
1 tablespoon minced shallots
1/2 cup minced celery
3/4 cup minced fresh parsley
2 tablespoons butter
3 cups brown chicken stock
3 cups diced potatoes
1/4 cup minced watercress
1 sprig thyme
2 cups sour cream
1/4 teaspoon salt
2 drops Tabasco sauce
1 large cucumber, peeled,
   seeded and coarsely grated
Half-and-half cream
Paprika
Minced fresh chives

Cook green onions, onion, shallots, celery and parsley in butter, covered, until vegetables are soft but not brown. Add stock, potatoes, watercress and thyme. Cover, bring to boil, lower heat and simmer until potatoes are soft.

Purée, cool and blend in sour cream, seasonings and cucumber. Chill.

Adjust seasonings and thin with cream, if needed. Sprinkle with paprika and chives.

VARIATION Garnish with extra watercress.

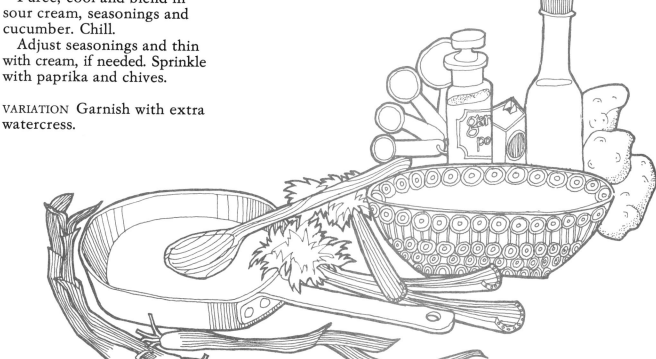

151

LOBSTER BISQUE

Serves 3 or 4
3 tablespoons chopped onion
2 tablespoons minced celery
1 tablespoon minced shallots
2 tablespoons butter
2 tablespoons unbleached
  flour
1-1/2 cups half-and-half
  cream
2 cups white chicken stock
1/4 cup dry white wine
1 tablespoon butter
One 8-ounce lobster tail,
  minced
1/4 cup brandy, heated
1/4 teaspoon salt
1/8 teaspoon white pepper
3 drops Tabasco sauce
Milk
Paprika
Minced fresh chives

Sauté onion, celery and shallots in butter 5 minutes, sprinkle with flour and cook, stirring, 3 minutes. Gradually add cream, stock and wine; cook and stir until smooth and slightly thickened.

Melt butter until bubbly, add lobster and cook rapidly, stirring, until lobster loses its translucent appearance. Pour brandy over, ignite and let burn down.

Combine lobster and juices with cream sauce, cover and simmer 10 minutes. Purée or sieve. Thin to desired consistency with milk, chill, adjust seasonings, and serve with a sprinkling of paprika and chives.

VARIATION Substitute flaked cooked crab meat for the lobster.

SHRIMP BISQUE

Serves 4 to 6
1-1/2 pounds shrimp, shelled
  and deveined
Fresh lemon juice
2 cups milk
1 cup half-and-half cream
1/4 cup *each* minced onion
  and celery
1/2 to 1 teaspoon anchovy
  paste
Bouquet garni of
  1 sprig thyme
  3 sprigs parsley
  6 black peppercorns,
    lightly crushed
  1 small bay leaf
1-1/2 tablespoons raw white
  rice
1 cup heavy cream
Tabasco sauce, salt, white
  pepper and Worcestershire
  sauce to taste
Pimiento strips

Cook 1/2 pound of the shrimp in rapidly boiling salted water with lots of lemon juice 2 to 3 minutes until pink; do not overcook. Dice and reserve.

Combine rest of shrimp, milk, half-and-half cream, onion, celery, anchovy paste, bouquet garni and rice. Cover, bring to gentle boil, lower heat and simmer 45 minutes, stirring occasionally.

Discard bouquet garni and purée. Add cream and chill. Adjust seasonings with Tabasco, salt, pepper and Worcestershire sauce and serve in chilled bowls. Garnish with reserved shrimp and pimiento strips.

VARIATION Sprinkle with minced fresh dill.

GAZPACHO

This version of gazpacho is very mild in comparison to many Spanish recipes. Increase the Tabasco, cumin and garlic for a spicier flavor.

Serves 6
2 cups gelatinous chicken
  stock
3 cups water
3 tablespoons chicken stock
  base
1 large red onion, sliced
4 garlic cloves
1/4 to 1/2 cup minced bell
  pepper
3 large tomatoes, peeled,
  seeded and finely minced
2 tablespoons finely minced
  bell pepper
2 cucumbers, peeled, seeded
  and finely minced
1 clove garlic, *finely* minced
1/4 cup finely minced celery
2 tablespoons finely minced
  red onion

1-1/2 tablespoons fresh
  lemon or lime juice
3 tablespoons olive oil
2 or 3 drops Tabasco sauce
  and/or 1/4 teaspoon
  ground cumin
Salt to taste
2 ripe avocados, cut in rings
2 cups herb croutons
Extra minced vegetables
Minced fresh chives and
  parsley

Bring stock, water, stock base, onion, whole garlic cloves and minced bell pepper to a boil, lower heat, cover and simmer gently for 10 minutes; cool, strain and chill.

Gently stir in tomatoes, finely minced bell pepper, cucumbers, minced garlic, celery, onion, lemon juice, olive oil and Tabasco. Chill thoroughly and adjust seasonings with salt.

Serve in large chilled bowls, with an ice cube if desired, and garnish with avocado rings and herb croutons. Pass extra minced vegetables, chives and parsley.

VARIATION Add cooked rice or French bread cubes that have been soaked in tomato juice and garlic and diced cooked shrimp. Season with white-wine vinegar to taste.

Hot or Cold

WATERCRESS SOUP

Serves 2 or 3

2 tablespoons minced onion
2 teaspoons butter
1-1/2 cups chopped water-
   cress, or 2 cups chopped
   curlycress leaves and tender
   stems
1-1/2 teaspoons unbleached
   flour
1/2 teaspoon chicken stock
   base
1/4 teaspoon *each* white
   pepper and garlic powder
1 egg
2 cups chicken or veal stock
1/2 cup half-and-half cream
1/2 cup heavy cream
Salt
Lemon slices
1 hard-cooked egg, sieved

Sauté onion in butter until soft. Purée with watercress, flour, stock base, pepper, garlic powder, raw egg and 1 cup of the stock.

Combine with rest of stock and half-and-half cream. Cook in double boiler or heavy saucepan 30 minutes, stirring occasionally. Add heavy cream.

Chill, adjust seasonings with salt and garnish with lemon slices and hard-cooked egg.

VARIATION To serve hot, re-heat without boiling, adjust seasonings with salt and gar-nish with lemon slices and watercress sprigs.

AVGOLEMONO
(Greek Lemon Soup)

Serves 6

2 tablespoons cornstarch
2 cups half-and-half cream
4 cups slightly gelatinous
   chicken stock
4 egg yolks, beaten
1/2 cup fresh lemon juice or
   to taste
Salt
White pepper
Thin lemon slices
Minced fresh parsley and/or
   chives

Mix cornstarch with a little of the cream; add to rest of cream. Add cream to stock; cook, stirring, until smooth and slightly thickened. Whisk 1/2 cup hot soup into egg yolks. Return to rest of soup, beating constantly, and add lemon juice. Adjust seasonings with salt and pepper to taste, strain through fine sieve and chill thoroughly.

Serve in chilled bowls with a garnish of thinly sliced lemon and minced parsley and/or chives.

VARIATION Heat but do not boil. Add 1 teaspoon freshly grated lemon peel and fold in the beaten whites of 2 eggs. Serve over hot rice.

ZUCCHINI PUREE

Serves 4

1-1/2 pounds zucchini, diced
  (4 cups)
1/2 cup diced onion
1/2 teaspoon sugar
1/4 teaspoon salt
1 to 2 tablespoons chopped
  fresh oregano
2 sprigs chervil
1 cup chicken stock
1 tablespoon butter
1 tablespoon unbleached
  flour
1-1/2 cups milk
1 cup heavy cream
Salt and white pepper to taste
Cooked crab legs or shrimp
Lemon slices
Chervil sprigs

Cook zucchini, onion, seasonings and herbs in stock until vegetables are tender. Strain, reserving the stock, and purée vegetables.

Melt butter until bubbly, add flour and cook, stirring, 3 minutes. Gradually add milk and the reserved stock; cook and stir until smooth and slightly thickened. Add purée, blend well and stir in heavy cream.

Cool, chill, adjust seasonings with salt and pepper and garnish with crab legs, lemon slices and chervil sprigs.

VARIATION To serve hot, thicken with 1 cup shelled green peas, cooked and puréed; substitute half-and-half cream for the heavy cream, and heat without boiling. Serve with lemon slices and garlic croutons.

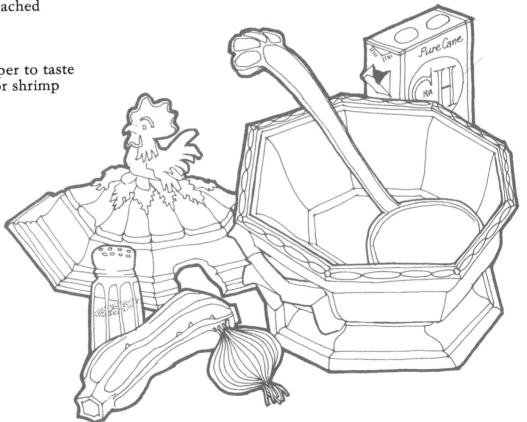

CREAMY SQUASH SOUP

Serves 4 to 6
2-1/2 to 3 cups diced
   yellow or banana squash
1-1/2 cups diced onion
1/2 cup diced celery
2 tablespoons diced carrot
1 teaspoon crumbled dried
   basil
1/4 teaspoon *each* sugar and
   white pepper
1/8 teaspoon *each* ground
   cloves and mace
1/2 teaspoon salt
2 tablespoons butter
2-1/2 cups chicken stock
1 cup half-and-half cream
1/2 cup heavy cream
Paprika
Minced fresh chives

Cook and stir vegetables,
herbs and seasonings in butter 10 minutes. Add stock,
cover, bring to boil, lower
heat and simmer until vegetables are tender.

Purée, add creams and heat;
do not boil. Cool, chill and
adjust seasonings.
   Sprinkle with paprika and
chives.

VARIATION To serve hot, heat
with a chiffonade of sorrel,
spinach and lettuce (page 172),
or add oysters frizzled in
butter and their own liquor.

POTATO-CELERY ROOT SOUP

Serves 4 to 6
1 cup *each* diced celery root
   and potato
1/2 cup minced onion
1/4 cup minced celery
2 tablespoons *each* minced
   leeks and fresh parsley
2 tablespoons butter
4 cups brown chicken or veal
   stock
1/4 teaspoon black pepper
2 bay leaves
2 egg yolks, beaten
1 cup half-and-half cream
1/2 cup heavy cream
Salt
Drained, minced capers

Sauté vegetables and parsley
in butter, stirring to coat
well, 5 minutes.
   Add stock, pepper and bay
leaves. Cover, bring to boil,
lower heat and simmer until
vegetables are soft. Discard
bay leaves and purée vegetable
mixture. Reheat.
   Beat together egg yolks and
half-and-half, whisk in 1/2
cup hot soup and return to
rest of soup. Cool, add heavy
cream and chill. Adjust seasonings with salt and garnish
with capers.

VARIATION To serve hot, omit
heavy cream and increase half-
and-half cream to 1-1/2 cups.
Garnish with minced celery
leaves.

---

*Watching calories? See page
186 for ideas on cream and
sour cream substitutes.*

CUCUMBER PUREE

Serves 6
3 large cucumbers, peeled, seeded and diced
1 large onion, diced
3 tablespoons butter
2-1/2 tablespoons unbleached flour
1/2 teaspoon paprika
1/4 teaspoon *each* white pepper and celery salt
1/4 teaspoon crumbled dried basil or thyme
5 cups brown chicken stock
1/2 tablespoon fresh lemon juice
2 tablespoons dry sherry or dry white wine
1 cup heavy cream
Salt
6 slices lemon
1/2 cup peeled, seeded and minced cucumber
2 tablespoons minced fresh dill

Sauté diced cucumbers and onion in butter until slightly browned. Sprinkle with flour and seasonings, cook, stirring, 3 minutes, and gradually add 2 cups of the stock. Cook and stir until smooth and slightly thickened. Cover and simmer 20 minutes.

Purée, add remaining stock, reheat to blend, cool, and add lemon juice, sherry and cream. Chill and adjust seasonings to taste with salt, lemon juice and wine. Garnish with lemon slices, minced cucumber and dill.

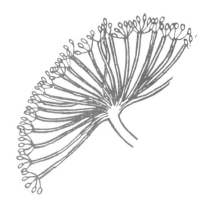

VARIATION To serve hot, omit heavy cream, add 1 cup half-and-half cream and heat without boiling. Adjust seasonings and garnish with sour cream whipped with a little soy sauce, lemon slices and finely minced bell pepper.

CARROT CREME

Serves 4 to 6
4 to 5 cups thinly sliced carrots
1/4 cup chopped onion
1/2 teaspoon *each* sugar and ground marjoram
1/4 teaspoon ground thyme
2 to 3 tablespoons butter and/or rendered chicken fat
1/4 cup raw brown rice
2 cups milk
1 bay leaf
4 cups chicken stock
1/2 cup heavy cream
Salt
Minced fresh mint

Cook carrots, onion and seasonings in butter, covered, until vegetables start to soften. Add brown rice and stir to coat, browning lightly. Add milk, bay leaf and 1 cup of the stock. Cover, bring to gentle boil, lower heat and simmer 30 minutes, stirring occasionally, or until rice is tender.

Discard bay leaf and purée. Add remaining stock and the cream. Reheat, but do not boil. Cool, chill and adjust seasonings with salt, sugar and/or marjoram. Garnish with mint.

VARIATION Serve hot with dry sherry to taste. Garnish with grated raw carrot and minced fresh chervil or watercress.

If blender or food processor does not purée finely enough, put through a sieve, ricer or food mill.

CREAM OF TOMATO SOUP

Serves 6

2 cups chopped fresh
    tomatoes
1/2 cup chopped celery with
    some leaves
1/4 cup *each* chopped carrot
    and onion
1 teaspoon sugar
4 large basil leaves
1 sprig parsley
1 sprig marjoram
1 bay leaf
3 tablespoons butter
1/2 cup chicken stock
2 tablespoons unbleached
    flour
2 cups half-and-half cream
1 tablespoon chicken stock
    base
1/4 teaspoon *each* paprika and
    white pepper
1/4 cup sour cream
Salt and minced fresh basil
    to taste
Diced ripe tomato, or 1/4
    cup mayonnaise seasoned
    to taste with curry powder
2 tablespoons minced fresh
    parsley

Cook chopped tomatoes, celery, carrot, onion, sugar, and herbs in 1 tablespoon of the butter, covered, until vegetables are soft. Discard herbs and force vegetables through food mill with stock. Melt remaining butter until bubbly, add flour and cook, stirring, 3 minutes. Gradually add cream; cook and stir until smooth and slightly thickened.

Add vegetable purée, stock base, paprika and pepper; simmer, stirring occasionally, 20 minutes.

Blend in sour cream and heat just to melt; do not boil. Cool, chill and adjust seasonings with salt and basil. Garnish with diced tomato and minced parsley.

VARIATION To serve hot, simply heat without boiling, adjust seasonings and garnish with minced artichoke hearts and a sprinkling of minced fresh basil.

Fruit Soups

Only the pure in heart can make a good soup.

—Beethoven, 1824

Fruit soups are especially popular in Germany as desserts and in the Scandinavian countries for breakfast and lunch. Fruit soups should all be icy cold and served in chilled bowls. Combinations of fresh and dried fruits offer varying degrees of sweetness and tartness. I've found that if a fruit soup is too syrupy or tart it's better to add light wine than more water. A dash of liqueur can add an interesting contrast, too.

To make a cornstarch binder, mix cornstarch with cold water, stir to dissolve thoroughly and then slowly add to soup, stirring in well.

MIXED FRUIT SOUP

Serves 6
4 cups diced fresh fruit
   (plums, apricots, cherries,
   apples, peaches)
3 cups water
3 tablespoons sugar
2 slices lemon
One 4-inch cinnamon stick
2 tablespoons raspberry juice
1/4 cup fresh orange juice
2 teaspoons fresh lemon juice
6 tablespoons port
Sugar
Whipped sour cream
Mint sprigs

Cook fruit, water, sugar, lemon slices and cinnamon, covered, until fruit is soft. Discard lemon and cinnamon; force fruit through sieve. Add juices and port; chill and adjust to taste with juice, sugar and/or port. Serve with dollops of sour cream and garnish with mint sprigs.

FRUIT BOUILLON

Serves 4
1 pound fresh bing cherries,
   pitted and chopped
6 tablespoons fresh orange
   juice
1-1/2 tablespoons fresh
   lemon juice
1/4 cup dry sherry
Rhine wine, well chilled
Sugar (optional)
Thin slices of orange and
   lemon

Purée 1/2 cup cherries with the orange juice. Combine with lemon juice and sherry. Add remainder of chopped cherries. Chill, add wine to taste and adjust, adding sugar if needed. Float orange and lemon slices on top.

GARLIC WITH FRUIT

Serves 4 to 6

3 to 5 garlic cloves, minced
1/3 cup slivered blanched
  almonds
3 slices white bread, crusts
  removed and diced
2-1/2 tablespoons olive oil
3-1/2 cups chicken or veal
  stock
1/4 teaspoon salt
1/8 teaspoon white pepper
2 tablespoons dry white wine
1/2 cup cantaloupe, crenshaw
  or honeydew melon balls,
  chilled
1 bunch seedless white grapes,
  chilled
1/4 pound prosciutto ham,
  torn into strips
Lightly toasted slivered
  almonds

Purée garlic and almonds, combine with bread and sauté in
oil until golden. Add stock,
salt and pepper and cook 10
minutes. Purée and cool. Add
wine, chill and adjust seasonings to taste. Garnish with
melon balls, grapes and ham
and pass toasted almonds.

SCANDINAVIAN FRUIT SOUP

Serves 8

1 package (12 ounce) mixed
  dried fruits
1/2 cup golden seedless raisins
2 tablespoons dried currants
5 cups water
1 orange, sliced 1/4 inch thick
1 lemon, sliced 1/4 inch thick
1/2 cup *each* currant jelly
  and sugar
2 tablespoons quick-cooking
  tapioca
1/4 teaspoon salt
2-1/2 cups unsweetened
  pineapple juice
1 cup peeled and diced apple
  (optional)

Combine fruits, raisins, currants and water. Cover, bring
to boil, lower heat and simmer
until tender. Add remaining
ingredients and simmer 10
minutes. Cool, chill and serve
with hard French rolls and
unsalted butter.

VARIATION Add 1/2 cup port,
or to taste, after cooling.

APPELSUPPE
Apple Soup

Serves 4 to 6

4 large tart apples, chopped
4 slices lemon
One 1-inch cinnamon stick
2-1/2 cups water
1/2 cup sour cream, whipped
  (at room temperature)
3 to 4 tablespoons extra-fine
  sugar
1-1/2 cups claret or rosé wine
1 to 2 teaspoons fresh lemon
  juice
Ground cinnamon
Mint sprigs

Cook apples, lemon and cinnamon stick in water until
apples are soft. Remove lemon
and cinnamon stick and sieve
apples, forcing as much pulp
through as possible. Beat 1/2
cup apple mixture with sour
cream and return to rest of
soup. Add sugar and blend
well. Gradually stir in wine,
add lemon juice and chill.
Adjust with more sugar, wine
and/or lemon juice. Sprinkle
with a little cinnamon and
serve with a garnish of mint
sprigs.

APRICOT WINE SOUP

Serves 6 to 8
2/3 cup chopped dried
    apricots
2/3 cup peeled and diced tart
    apple
1 cup water
1 can (12 ounce) apricot-
    orange nectar
1-1/4 cups apple juice
1/2 cup sour cream
3/4 cup chilled dry white
    wine, or to taste
Mint sprigs

Cook apricots and apple in
water, covered, until apricots
are soft, adding more water if
needed. Purée with nectar,
apple juice and sour cream.
Chill, add wine and serve with
mint sprigs.

VARIATION For extra bite, add
a few drops of Tabasco sauce.

COLD CHERRY SOUP

Serves 6 to 8
2-1/4 cups water
3/4 cup extra-fine sugar
One 3-inch cinnamon stick
4 cups pitted sour cherries,
    or 2 cans (1 pound *each*)
    water-pack sour cherries,
    drained
1 tablespoon cornstarch,
    mixed with 2 tablespoons
    water
1/4 cup *each* dry red wine and
    heavy cream
1/2 cup Cherry Heering, or
    to taste, well chilled
Minced fresh mint
Whipped sour cream

Bring water, sugar, cinnamon
and cherries to boil. Lower
heat and simmer 30 minutes
for fresh, 10 minutes for
canned. Stir cornstarch binder
into cherries and cook and
stir until clear and slightly
thickened. Remove about a
cup of cherries and some
juice; purée and return to
rest of soup. Cool, add wine
and cream, blend and chill
thoroughly.

Just before serving, add
chilled Cherry Heering to taste.
Garnish with mint and dollops
of whipped sour cream.

CANTALOUPE SOUP

Serves 4
1 large cantaloupe, seeded
    and diced
5 tablespoons butter
2 teaspoons sugar
1 teaspoon freshly grated
    lemon peel
Pinch *each* ground ginger
    and salt
2-1/2 cups milk
Fresh lemon juice and/or
    white rum
Mint sprigs

Reserve 1 cup diced cantaloupe (or scoop out balls) for
garnish. Cook remainder in
butter with sugar, lemon peel,
ginger and salt, covered, until
soft. Add milk, bring to boil,
lower heat and simmer 10
minutes.

Purée, cool and chill. Adjust
seasonings with lemon juice.
Garnish with reserved cantaloupe and mint.

TOMATO-ORANGE SOUP

Serves 4 to 6
2 cups *each* tomato and
  orange juice
2 tablespoons fresh lemon
  juice
1/2 cup dry white wine
1/4 teaspoon minced fresh
  basil
Salt, cayenne pepper and
  black pepper to taste
Whipped cream
Minced fresh chives

Combine juices, wine and
basil. Chill, adjust with salt
and peppers. Garnish with
dollops of whipped cream and
minced chives.

PLUM SOUP

Serves 3 or 4
1-1/2 cups chopped ripe
  plums
1/4 cup crumbled rusks
1/2 cup *each* dry white wine
  and apple juice
Small pinch *each* ground
  cinnamon, cloves and ginger
2 tablespoons heavy cream
1 teaspoon sugar
1/2 teaspoon fresh lemon
  juice
1/4 cup Rhine wine
Unpeeled apple slices, rubbed
  with fresh lemon juice

Cook plums, rusk crumbs,
wine, apple juice and spices
until plums are soft. Sieve.
  Add cream, sugar, lemon
juice and wine. Chill and
adjust seasonings to taste,
adding more chilled wine if
desired. Garnish with apple
slices.

BRANDIED PEACH
AND PLUM SOUP

Serves 6
2 cups *each* diced fresh
  peaches and plums
1-1/2 cups *each* water and dry
  red wine
2/3 cup sugar
1 slice lemon
One 4-inch cinnamon stick
2 tablespoons cognac
Finely minced fresh mint

Cook peaches, plums, water,
wine, sugar, lemon and cinnamon, covered, until fruits are
soft. Discard lemon and cinnamon; force fruits through
sieve. Add cognac, chill and
adjust to taste, adding sugar
and/or cognac as needed. Garnish with mint.

STRAWBERRY-WINE SOUP

Serves 4

2 cups sliced fresh
  strawberries
6 tablespoons sugar
1 cup water
2 teaspoons cornstarch,
  mixed with 1 tablespoon
  water
1 cup dry white wine
1 to 2 tablespoons fresh
  lemon juice
2 teaspoons freshly grated
  lemon peel
Cognac
Lemon peel strips

Combine strawberries, sugar and water; simmer until berries are soft. Stir in cornstarch binder and cook and stir until thickened. Purée. Add wine, lemon juice and lemon peel. Chill and adjust with lemon juice, wine and cognac. Garnish with tiny lemon peel strips.

VARIATION Add 1/4 cup sour cream when puréeing.

165

RHUBARB FRUIT SOUP

Serves 6 to 8
3/4 cup extra-fine sugar
4 cups water
One 3-inch cinnamon stick
3/4 cup quartered dried
     apricots
2-1/2 to 3 cups diced rhubarb
2 tablespoons cornstarch,
     mixed with 3 tablespoons
     water or raspberry juice
1 package (10 ounce) frozen
     raspberries, thawed and
     drained
1 tablespoon fresh lemon
     juice
Sugar to taste
Freshly grated orange peel
Sliced strawberries

Combine sugar, water, cinnamon and apricots. Cover,
bring to boil, lower heat and
simmer 5 minutes. Add rhubarb, bring back to boil and
simmer until rhubarb is barely
tender.

Add cornstarch binder to
fruit; cook and stir until slightly
thickened and clear. Add rasp-
berries and lemon juice; adjust
with sugar. Chill. Garnish with
orange peel and strawberries.

RASPBERRY SOUP

Serves 6
1 package (10 ounce) package
     frozen raspberries, thawed
1 can (11 ounce) mandarin
     orange segments and juice
1/2 cup fresh orange juice
1/4 cup dry red wine
1/4 cup fresh lemon juice
1 cup dry white wine
1 tablespoon kirsch
Sugar (optional)
Finely minced fresh mint
Mint sprigs

Combine all ingredients, except mint sprigs, and chill
thoroughly. Garnish with mint
sprigs.

ICY WATERMELON SOUP

Serves 6
1/2 medium watermelon
1 to 1-1/2 cups Rhine wine
2/3 cup sugar
3/4 cup water
4 slices lemon or lime
One 2-inch piece vanilla bean
Finely minced fresh mint

Scoop 12 balls from seedless
portion of watermelon. Combine with wine and chill. Cube
remaining watermelon, remove
seeds and set aside.

Simmer sugar, water, lemon
slices and vanilla bean, covered,
20 minutes. Discard lemon
slices and vanilla bean.

Put 2 cups watermelon
cubes in blender or food processor; pour in sugar water
and blend until smooth. Chill,
combine with melon balls and
wine and adjust to taste.
Sprinkle with mint.

Accoutrements

"Beautiful soup! Who cares for fish
Game, or any other dish?
Who would not give all else for two
Pennyworth only of beautiful soup?"
　　　　　　　—Alice in Wonderland

ACCOUTREMENTS

A soup is not the beautiful soup Alice in Wonderland extolls without a pretty serving bowl, attractive table or tray settings and appropriate individual dishes. Colorful and tasty trimmings of various shapes and sizes, some in the soup itself, others alongside on the plate, add pleasure to both the eye and the tongue.

Cook and try a dumpling or meatball first so you can adjust seasonings to your taste before cooking the entire batch.

Colorful, tasty garnishes can turn a simple soup into a spectacular one.

CREPES

1 egg
1-1/2 tablespoons milk
1 tablespoon unbleached flour
1/8 teaspoon salt
1 tablespoon finely minced fresh parsley or chives (optional)
Butter

Beat together egg, milk and flour until smooth. Add salt and parsley, cover and refrigerate several hours.

Heat a 7-inch skillet over medium heat and add butter to coat. Adding additional milk if too thick, pour in half the batter. Tip pan to evenly coat surface and cook until lightly brown. Turn and lightly brown other side. Transfer to cooling rack. Repeat with remaining batter. Cool, roll and cut into strips. Serve in clear soups.

ROYALES

1 cup chicken, veal or beef stock
1 garlic clove, minced
2 large sprigs parsley
1 sprig savory or oregano
1/4 teapoon paprika
2 eggs
2 egg yolks
1/4 cup any ground cooked vegetable, meat, poultry or game (optional)

Simmer stock, garlic, herbs and paprika 10 minutes. Strain and cool. Beat together eggs and egg yolks and beat in stock. Sieve into buttered 7- or 8-inch square pan and stir in ground vegetable. Bake in 350° oven 20 minutes or until knife inserted in center comes out clean. Cool, chill and cut into squares or other decorative shapes. Serve in clear soups.

EGG DUMPLINGS

Makes approximately 25
6 hard-cooked egg yolks
1/2 teaspoon unbleached
  flour, or as needed
2 eggs, beaten
1 teaspoon salt
1/8 teaspoon white pepper
1/8 teaspoon curry powder
  or freshly grated nutmeg

Mash together cooked yolks and flour and mix in raw eggs and seasonings, adding more flour to make a workable dough. Form into small balls and drop into gently boiling salted water. Cook 5 minutes or until balls rise to surface.

POTATO DUMPLINGS

Makes 25 to 30
3 medium baking potatoes
2 eggs, lightly beaten
1/2 teaspoon salt
1/4 teaspoon ground thyme
1/8 teaspoon white pepper
1 tablespoon *finely* minced
  parsley
1/4 cup unbleached
  flour, or as needed

Boil potatoes in their skins until tender. Cool and refrigerate several hours or overnight. Peel and grate to measure approximately 2-1/2 to 3 cups. With fork, stir in eggs, seasonings and parsley. Then stir in flour, adding additional flour as needed to make a workable but not heavy mixture. Adjust seasonings and form into balls the size of large marbles. Drop into gently boiling salted water, 10 or 12 at a time. Cook at gentle boil until dumplings rise to surface, remove with slotted spoon and keep warm. Repeat with remaining dumpling mixture.

NOTE Save potato water for making stock. Use within 48 hours.

EGG FOAM DUMPLINGS

Makes approximately 12
1 egg, separated
1/4 teaspoon salt
1/8 teaspoon freshly grated
  nutmeg
1 tablespoon *each* freshly
  grated Parmesan cheese
  and fine bread crumbs

Combine egg yolk, seasonings, cheese and bread crumbs. Beat egg white until stiff but not dry. Gently fold a small portion of egg white into yolk mixture. Then fold into remaining egg white. Drop by tablespoonfuls into broth kept at slow boil. Simmer 5 minutes.

BUTTER DUMPLINGS

Makes approximately 20
1 egg, beaten
3-1/2 tablespoons softened
  butter
1/8 teaspoon salt
Dash *each* celery salt, paprika
  and ground thyme
1 teaspoon finely minced
  fresh parsley
1/2 teaspoon finely minced
  fresh chives
5-1/2 tablespoons unbleached
  flour

Mix together egg, butter, seasonings and herbs. Stir in
flour and let stand at room
temperature 1 hour. Drop by
teaspoonfuls into gently boiling salted water or broth.
They are cooked when they
rise to the surface.

MARROW DUMPLINGS

Makes approximately 20
Two 3-inch marrow bones
1-1/2 tablespoons softened
  butter
1 egg, beaten
1 tablespoon minced fresh
  parsley
6 tablespoons fine bread
  crumbs
1/4 teaspoon *each* salt and
  baking powder
1/8 teaspoon *each* black
  pepper and freshly grated
  nutmeg

Remove marrow from bones
to make 3 tablespoons. Mash
with fork and mix in butter.
Combine with remaining ingredients and form into small
balls the size of a nutmeg.
Drop into gently boiling water
and cook about 5 minutes
until balls are slightly puffed
and rise to surface. Be careful
not to overcook.

ALMOND DUMPLINGS

Makes approximately 30
1 cup finely crushed unsalted
  cracker crumbs
1/2 cup blanched whole
  almonds, coarsely ground
1/2 cup milk
1 egg, beaten
3 tablespoons browned butter
1/4 teaspoon salt
1/8 teaspoon *each* white
  pepper and garlic powder
1/4 teaspoon freshly grated
  lemon peel
Unbleached flour, if needed

Mix together all ingredients,
chill and form into small
balls, using flour if needed to
make a workable dough. Drop
by half teaspoonfuls into gently
boiling salted water or broth;
cook 5 minutes or until balls
rise to surface.

BREAD DUMPLINGS

Makes 24
2 eggs, beaten
3/4 cup fine bread crumbs, or
   as needed
1/2 teapoon cornstarch
1 teaspoon milk
2 teaspoons finely minced
   fresh parsley
1/4 teaspoon salt
1/4 teaspoon freshly grated
   lemon peel
1 teaspoon grated onion

Mix together all ingredients,
using more bread crumbs if
needed to make a workable
dough. Chill at least 1 hour.
Form into 24 small balls and
cook in simmering salted
water 3 minutes after balls
rise to the surface and puff
up.

CHICKEN BALLS

Makes approximately 40
1-1/2 cups ground white
   chicken meat
2 tablespoons finely minced
   fresh parsley
1 egg, beaten
1/2 cup fine bread crumbs
1 tablespoon freshly grated
   Romano cheese
1/4 teaspoon *each* salt and
   black pepper

Mix together all ingredients,
form into balls the size of
large marbles and refrigerate
several hours. Cook in simmering salted water or broth
10 minutes.

FORCEMEAT BALLS

Makes approximately 25
2 hard-cooked egg yolks
1 teaspoon milk
3 tablespoons fine bread
   crumbs
1/2 cup ground cooked meat,
   poultry or game
1 egg, beaten
1 teaspoon unbleached flour
1/4 teaspoon salt
1/8 teaspoon white pepper

Mash egg yolks with milk and
mix with remaining ingredients. Flour hands and form
small balls the size of a nutmeg. Drop into gently boiling
water or broth and cook until
they rise to the surface.

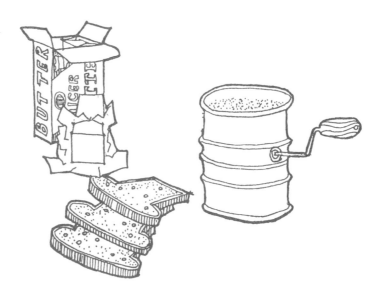

Garnitures

CHIFFONADE

Sauté 1/2 cup chopped sorrel, spinach, lettuce, kale or any leafy vegetable or combination, in 2 tablespoons butter.

AIOLI SAUCE

Purée 2 to 4 garlic cloves, minced, 1 egg yolk, 1/4 teaspoon salt and 1 teaspoon fresh lemon juice in blender or processor. Turn on high and in a steady stream, add 2/3 cup olive oil. Adjust seasonings with salt and white pepper.

ANCHOVY-EGG SAUCE

Mix together 3 hard-cooked eggs, sieved, 1-1/2 teaspoons heavy cream, 1 to 1-1/2 teaspoons anchovy paste, 2 drops Tabasco sauce, 1/2 teaspoon Worcestershire sauce and 3 to 4 tablespoons mayonnaise. Adjust to taste.

BROILED CREAM

Whip 1/2 cup heavy cream until stiff. If desired, fold in 2 tablespoons freshly grated Parmesan cheese. To use, spoon on top of soup in 6 ovenproof bowls. Set 6 inches below heat and broil 1 minute. Watch carefully!

MINCED FRESH HERBS AND SPICES chives, dill, coriander, chervil, parsley, Italian parsley, rosemary, mint, fennel, green onions, celery leaves, watercress, lovage, borage

BLANCHED OR BROWNED VEGETABLE DICE OR JULIENNE celery root, beets, carrots, turnips, potatoes, artichoke hearts, asparagus tips, red onions, celery, green or red bell peppers, green beans, leeks, mushrooms, spinach

JULIENNED OR DICED UNCOOKED VEGETABLES radishes, red or green bell peppers, carrots, celery, avocados, tomatoes, mushrooms, cucumbers, garlic

GRATED UNCOOKED VEGETABLES carrots, celery root, zucchini, sunchokes, jicama, beets

CITRUS fruit, sliced; peel, grated or cut into curls or tiny strips

OTHERS popcorn; slivered toasted almonds; chopped, sliced or sieved hard-cooked eggs; sour cream beaten with soy sauce, paprika or caviar; heavy cream whipped with soy sauce or paprika; grated cheeses; cheese balls (Gorgonzola or cream cheese) rolled in paprika; pork or bacon cracklings; sliced cooked sausages; cooked rice and pastas; sliced olives

---

Some soup garnitures also make delicious toppings for steamed vegetables. Try Aioli Sauce, Anchovy-Egg Sauce, Pistou.

CROUTONS

In a 200° oven, dry sliced whole wheat, white, pumpernickel, rye, French or Italian bread, cut into 1/2-inch squares. Toss 3 cups of the bread squares with 1/4 cup melted butter mixed with one of the following mixtures. Brown in a 300° oven, stirring often.
- 1/4 cup freshly grated Parmesan cheese, 1/2 teaspoon paprika, dash cayenne pepper
- 1/2 teaspoon salt, 1 to 2 teaspoons mixed ground herbs, black pepper
- 1-1/2 tablespoons fresh lemon juice, 1 teaspoon freshly grated lemon peel, 1/2 teaspoon paprika
- salt and cayenne pepper
- 2 garlic cloves, pressed, 1/2 teaspoon crumbled dried oregano, salt, black pepper
- 2 tablespoons freshly grated Parmesan cheese, 1/2 teaspoon paprika, 1/2 teaspoon garlic powder, 1/2 teaspoon onion juice

Accompaniments

Serve whole-grain, French or rye breads, rolls, crackers or toasted English muffins as an accompaniment, or prepare one of the following.

BREAD FINGERS, ROUNDS, SQUARES, TRIANGLES, RINGS

Thinly slice whole-wheat, white, rye, French, Italian or pumpernickel bread, remove the crusts and allow to dry 1 day. Then top with one of the following and bake in a 200° oven for 1 hour or until crisp and dry.

- melted butter mixed with curry powder
- melted butter mixed with freshly grated Parmesan cheese and paprika
- melted butter, sprinkling of poppy, caraway or sesame seeds
- melted butter blended with minced fresh chives and/or parsley and minced fresh oregano, basil or tarragon
- butter melted with pressed garlic cloves, Worcestershire sauce and a pinch of salt
- melted butter mixed with fresh lemon juice and freshly grated lemon peel; sprinkling of paprika

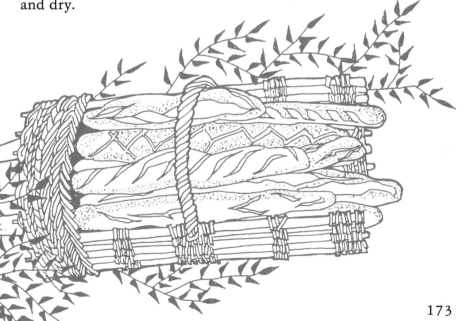

Mini Recipes

The tendency of modern dinners is to shorten the service; where but lately two soups were considered imperatively necessary one now suffices, . . .

—*Mrs. A. B. Marshall, circa 1898*

Only if time is very short or your larder is low should you take advantage of factory-prepared foods. They are uneconomical and often contain additives, preservatives and have a high salt content, all deleterious to good dietary habits. If you do choose to use commercial products, there are many ways of adding a personal touch that will improve a "factory soup."

The following recipe ideas are designed for canned soups in 10-1/2- or 11-ounce size. Check the section on garnitures for other ideas.

• Add 1/8 teaspoon crumbled dried basil and 1/4 cup dry red wine or Madeira to black bean soup. Garnish with lemon slices.

• Combine 1 can *each* cream of tomato and black bean soup with 1-1/2 soup cans water. Heat and serve topped with grated onion and lemon slices.

• Substitute 1/2 cup rosé wine for part of the water to be mixed with cream of chicken soup. Garnish with lime slices.

• Lace beef or chicken broth with dry sherry. Sprinkle with minced fresh chives or shredded Cheddar cheese.

• Combine and heat 1 can *each* cream of mushroom and cream of asparagus soup, 1 cup *each* milk and half-and-half cream and 1 cup flaked crab meat. Just before serving, add 1/4 cup dry sherry and 2 tablespoons butter.

• Combine and heat 3 cans cream of celery soup, 2-1/2 soup cans half-and-half cream, 1 cup chopped cooked shrimp or lobster and 1/2 cup shredded mild Cheddar cheese. Garnish with sliced black or stuffed olives.

• Simmer 3 cans beef consommé and 1 soup can water with 12 parsley sprigs 30 minutes. Discard parsley, chill until firm and break up with fork. Serve in chilled bowls with garnish of sour cream and black caviar.

• Purée 1 cup tomato juice, 3 tablespoons minced fresh parsley, 3 tablespoons minced onion, 1 ripe tomato, peeled and diced, 3 tablespoons sour cream and 1/2 can beef consommé. Chill, stir and season with Tabasco and Worcestershire sauce.

• Purée 2 cups diced peeled and seeded cucumber, 3 green onions, 2 tablespoons minced fresh parsley, 1 tablespoon minced fresh dill, 2 cups buttermilk and 1/4 cup sour cream. Chill. Season with salt, serve in chilled bowls and pass the peppermill.

• Combine and heat 1-1/2 cups chicken broth and 1/2 cup clam juice. Season to taste with dry sherry, salt and white pepper. Garnish with lemon peel or tiny spinach leaves.

• Combine and heat 1 can tomato bisque, 1 soup can milk and curry powder and ground cumin to taste. Garnish with dollops of plain yoghurt.

175

• Heat 1-1/2 cups vegetable juice, 1/2 cup pineapple juice, 1/2 teaspoon Worcestershire sauce and 3 drops Tabasco sauce. Sprinkle with minced fresh chives or bell pepper.

• Sauté 1/4 cup minced onion in 2 tablespoons butter until soft. Add and heat 2 cans cream of vegetable soup, 1-1/2 soup cans milk and 1 cup minced cooked shrimp. Add 1 large ripe tomato, peeled and diced; reheat briefly and sprinkle with minced fresh dill.

• Follow package directions for dry leek and onion soup; add 1 can minced clams and liquor. Reheat and garnish with finely minced garlic.

• Combine 1 can beef consommé or madrilène, 1/2 cup diced cooked shrimp, 1/4 cup minced celery, 2 tablespoons chopped watercress and black pepper to taste. Chill until firm, break up with fork and serve with lemon wedges and watercress sprigs.

• Heat 1 can madrilène and 2 tablespoons dry sherry. Cool, chill until firm and serve with avocado rings.

• Purée 1 can *each* oyster stew and cream of mushroom soup. Combine and heat with 2 cups milk. Cool, chill and serve in chilled bowls, garnished with chopped or sieved hard-cooked eggs and minced fresh parsley.

• Combine and heat 1 can *each* cream of chicken and cream of celery soup and 2 soup cans milk. Cool, chill and garnish with chopped peeled and seeded cucumber, chopped fresh mint or celery leaves.

• Season beef consommé with fresh lemon juice. Add dry white wine just before serving and garnish with lemon slices.

• Purée 2 cups chilled tomato juice, 1/2 teaspoon salt, 1/4 teaspoon *each* black pepper and crumbled dried basil, 1/8 teaspoon ground marjoram and 1/3 cup sour cream. Chill and garnish with minced fresh chives and lemon slices.

• Heat equal amounts of clam and tomato juice. Garnish with lime slices.

• Combine and heat 1 can condensed cream of mushroom soup, 1 can condensed chicken vegetable soup, 1 soup can water and one 12-ounce can whole kernel corn, drained. Add 1/2 cup *each* half-and-half cream and dry sherry. Sprinkle with crumbled cooked bacon and minced fresh parsley.

• Boil 1/2 cup raw rice in 5 cups chicken stock 15 to 20 minutes. Beat 2 egg yolks with 1/2 cup heavy cream, whisk in 1/2 cup hot soup and return to rest of soup. Reheat without boiling and add 2 to 3 tablespoons port. Sprinkle with minced fresh parsley.

• Heat beef consommé with chopped celery stalks and leaves 20 minutes. Strain and serve with minced celery and paprika.

• Combine and heat 1 can cream of mushroom soup, 1 can cream-style corn and 1-1/2 cups milk. Garnish with red bell pepper slivers.

• Combine and heat 1 can *each* New England clam chowder and chicken gumbo and 1-1/2 cans milk or cream. Garnish with minced fresh chives and paprika.

• Combine 2 cans beef consommé, 3/4 cup minced cooked shrimp, 1/4 cup thinly sliced celery, 2 tablespoons *each* minced fresh parsley and watercress and 1/8 teaspoon white pepper. Chill and garnish with lime wedges, extra whole shrimp and minced fresh parsley.

• Purée 1 can *each* cream of mushroom and cream of chicken soup, 1 small can mushrooms, drained, one 10-1/2-ounce package frozen chopped spinach, thawed, 2 teaspoons dried onion flakes and 1/4 teaspoon minced garlic. Combine and heat with 2-1/2 cups milk and salt and black pepper to taste. Garnish with sliced hard-cooked eggs and paprika.

• Blend 3 eggs, 1/4 cup dry sherry, 1/8 teaspoon freshly grated nutmeg and 2 tablespoons fresh lemon or lime juice. Slowly pour in 5 cups hot chicken broth and blend 1 minute. Garnish with minced fresh chervil and diced artichoke heart.

• Serve jellied beef consommé or madrilène with crumbled Roquefort cheese and minced chives.

• Purée one 10-1/2-ounce package frozen chopped spinach, thawed and drained, 3 cans vichysoisse, 2 teaspoons chicken stock base, 1 teaspoon onion powder, 1/4 teaspoon garlic powder and 1/2 cup milk. Season with salt and white pepper and serve with sieved hard-cooked eggs or grated cucumber.

• Combine 1 can cream of tomato soup, 1 cup milk, 1/2 cup heavy cream, 2/3 cup cream-style cottage cheese, 1/2 teaspoon Worcestershire sauce, and Tabasco sauce and salt to taste. Chill, adjust seasoning and serve in chilled bowls, garnished with slivered green onions.

• Purée 1 can cream of celery soup, 1 cup milk, 1/2 cup heavy cream, 2 cups firmly packed watercress leaves and some stems and 1 cup chopped peeled and seeded cucumber. Add salt to taste, chill, adjust seasoning and serve in chilled bowls, garnished with minced watercress.

• Heat 6 cups chicken broth, 1/4 teaspoon freshly grated lime peel and 3 tablespoons fresh lime juice. Garnish with lime slices.

• Combine and heat 1 can *each* cream of vegetable, pea and tomato soup and 2 cups milk. Garnish with pimiento slivers.

Waste Not, Want Not

Men are divided between those who are as
thrifty as if they would live forever,
and those who are as extravagant as if
they were going to die the next day.

                             —*Aristotle*

LEFTOVERS

Making soup is one of the best ways to use cooked and uncooked leftovers that are cluttering up your refrigerator. Here are some suggestions for using them.

• Shred lettuce or other leafy greens or chop broccoli, cauliflower or carrots. Cook, covered, in butter until soft. Purée, thin with stock and/or milk, half-and-half cream or heavy cream and season as desired.

• Sauté ground raw meat and add to soup at end of cooking period. Especially good in Tomato-Mushroom, Lentil, and Millet-Vegetable Soup.

• Make croutons from bread that has gone stale (page 173).

• Use extra milk, half-and-half cream or heavy cream for making cream soups.

• Save fat from raw meat or poultry and render it. Rendered chicken fat is especially good for sautéing soup vegetables before stock is added or for browning ingredients for brown stocks. Freeze rendered fat in individual ice cube holders or small containers and defrost as needed.

• If cheese is beginning to mold, grate and freeze it for adding to soups.

• When your green bean crop has stopped producing and pods you overlooked at harvest have withered on the vine, pick and shuck them and store the beans in the refrigerator in a jar with a tight-fitting lid. Add to soups 3 minutes before cooking period is finished. An unusual, delightful texture.

• Save bones and scraps (ask your butcher for those bones he cut from your roast) for making stocks. Freeze them if you aren't ready to use them right away.

• When your dinner roast is cooked, deglaze the roasting pan and add scrapings and some water to a small pot with the bones from the roast, if any. Simmer for 2 to 3 hours, adding whatever vegetables may be on hand for flavor. A great fortifier for your stocks.

• Noodle and rice casserole leftovers, especially those prepared with spinach or Swiss chard, can be added to stock for a quick lunch or dinner soup.

• Add cooked grains or pasta to soup at end of cooking period.

• Add cooked legumes to soup at end of cooking period. Or purée, thin with a little stock and season to taste. You can also freeze the purée in individual ice cube holders or small containers, then defrost and add to soup for flavor.

• Steam chopped onions or white of leeks in rendered chicken fat and/or butter until soft. Add leftover cooked vegetables and stir to coat. Purée with stock and reheat with milk, half-and-half cream and/or heavy cream. Season to taste with white or black pepper, ground herbs and salt.

• Use your imagination and combine leftover soups, adding herbs and seasonings, dry red wine or vermouth and fresh lemon juice to taste.

• Recycle your New England boiled dinner (but be sure to blanch and rinse the corned beef before you make it). Purée leftover cooked vegetables with the cooking liquid (not the meat or beets), heat and season with white pepper and ground herbs of choice. Add shredded leftover corned beef, if desired. Garnish with grated raw vegetables and minced fresh parsley.

• Last night's vegetable dish can easily become tonight's soup. Finely chop or purée Swiss chard that has been cooked in garlic and olive oil. Place in a pan, sprinkle with rice flour and season with soy sauce, ground ginger, white pepper and salt. Heat, thin with stock and plain yoghurt and add dry sherry to taste. Or purée sliced yellow zucchini that has been sautéed in butter with sliced red onions. Place in a pan, heat and thin with chicken stock and half-and-half cream and/or sour cream. Serve hot or cold.

• Save your vegetable cooking water and add to soups for added flavor and nutrition.

Watching calories? See page 186 for ideas on cream and sour cream substitutes.

CONSERVING ENERGY

You can conserve energy by cooking double the amount of an ingredient called for in a recipe, and using half of it to make a second soup. This is especially true of dried legumes.

For example, when precooking lima beans for Dried Lima Bean and Corn Soup, double the bean and water measurements. Remove half of the beans for the recipe and cook the remaining beans, adding additional water, 2 teaspoons chicken stock base, onion and garlic, until beans are very soft. Purée, cool, jar and freeze. When ready to use, defrost, reheat and add 1/2 cup each milk and half-and-half cream or heavy cream. Season to taste with salt, white pepper and cayenne pepper. Garnish with peeled and diced ripe tomato.

FREEZING VEGETABLES

During those seasons when the bounty from your garden is just too large to eat as it is picked or when sales at the local farmers' or produce market are too good to pass up, freeze the surplus to enjoy during the year. Here are some tips on how to freeze specific vegetables that are not commonly relegated to the home deep freeze. Unless otherwise stated, only freeze for up to one season.

ARTICHOKES Cook as directed in Artichoke Soup. Scrape edible pulp from leaves and trim and chop hearts. Freeze in tightly secured plastic bags for up to two months.

GREEN OR RED BELL PEPPERS Mince or chop and cook, covered, in butter and/or rendered chicken fat until almost tender. Freeze in small portions in tightly secured plastic bags.

CITRUS PEEL Freeze citrus peels in tightly secured plastic bags for up to three months. Defrost, then grate in blender or food processor.

CITRUS JUICE Freeze freshly squeezed citrus juice in individual ice cube holders or small containers for up to five months. (The flavor of frozen and thawed juice will not be as good as freshly squeezed juice.)

CORN Cut kernels off cooked corn on the cob and freeze in airtight containers. (To make a slightly cream-style corn, slit each row down the center with a sharp knife to open the kernels, then cut the kernels from the cob. Finally, scrape the rows with the back of a knife to release any remaining milky residue.) Use as you would canned corn.

LEEKS OR GREEN ONIONS Chop white and green parts separately and cook separately, covered, in butter and/or rendered chicken fat just until soft. Freeze in tightly secured plastic bags for up to six months.

YELLOW OR WHITE ONIONS Peel, mince and cook, covered, in butter and/or rendered chicken fat just until soft. Freeze in tightly secured plastic bags for up to six months.

SUMMER SQUASH Because of high-water content, it is necessary to grate the squash before freezing in airtight containers. You may also cook the grated squash with desired seasonings, purée and freeze the purée for up to six months.

SWISS CHARD, SPINACH, BEET GREENS AND OTHER LEAFY GREENS Using only the water that clings to the leaves after washing, cook until moisture has evaporated in a little olive oil seasoned with whole or crushed garlic cloves. Form the cooked greens into a ball and freeze in tightly secured plastic bags for up to six months.

TOMATOES Place unpeeled whole tomatoes in plastic bags and secure tightly closed. When ready to use, remove from the freezer and spread out on a kitchen surface. Let them defrost at room temperature until the peels come off easily, being careful not to let them get too soft before proceeding with this step. Once the tomatoes are peeled and stemmed, chop them and use in place of canned tomatoes in soups, or for making tomato juice, sauce, paste or catsup.

Here are two soups that use the surplus you froze at the height of the season.

CORN AND TOMATO BISQUE

Serves 2

3 tablespoons minced onion
1 small garlic clove, minced
1 tablespoon rendered chicken fat and/or butter
1 cup milk
2 large frozen tomatoes, partially thawed, peeled and chopped
1 bay leaf
1/2 teaspoon crumbled dried oregano
Pinch sugar or to taste
Dash black pepper
1 cup frozen cooked corn kernels, thawed
Salt to taste
Minced fresh parsley
Croutons

Cook onion and garlic in chicken fat, covered, until soft. Add milk, tomatoes, herbs and seasonings. Cover, bring to gentle boil, lower heat and simmer 15 minutes. Discard bay leaf. Add corn kernels, reheat and season with salt. Garnish with parsley and pass the croutons.

VARIATION Add 1/4 cup frozen chopped bell pepper with the corn. Garnish with freshly grated Parmesan cheese.

SURPLUS-ARTICHOKE SOUP

3 tablespoons minced onion
2 teaspoons rendered chicken fat and/or butter
2 cups frozen minced cooked artichoke hearts and pulp scraped from leaves, thawed
Chicken stock
Half-and-half and/or heavy cream
Salt, white pepper and fresh lemon juice to taste
Minced fresh parsley and/or chives

Sauté onion in fat just until golden. Purée with artichoke and a little stock, if needed. Heat with cream to taste, thinning if needed with additional stock. Season with salt, pepper and lemon juice. Garnish with parsley.

DEHYDRATING FRUITS AND VEGETABLES

There are a number of home dehydrating units presently on the market that are ideal for drying any vine-ripened fruits and vegetables. These units are particularly attractive to those with limited freezer space, since the dried produce can be stored in airtight containers in any cool place.

Complete directions come with any unit you purchase. It is important that you select unblemished, ripe fruits and vegetables for drying, and that you slice them uniformly. Dehydrated fruits can be used to make fruit soups, and dehydrated vegetables, such as tomatoes, onions, celery and mushrooms, are excellent for making vegetable and meat soups and stocks.

Dehydrated vegetables are handy for the camper or backpacker. Finely chop the vegetables before drying them, pack in plastic bags and enjoy a delicious soup on the trail or at the campsite.

Dried vegetables may also be pulverized in a blender or processor and added to soups and stocks for a concentrated flavoring. These vegetable powders can be stored, refrigerated, for no more than three weeks. Mushrooms prepared in this manner may be substituted for dried mushrooms in mushroom concentrate (page 14), but reduce the measurement by half. Powdered mushrooms are also good sprinkled on oxtails when browning them for soup, and added to soups *in addition* to mushroom concentrate to intensify the mushroom flavor.

Always reconstitute dried vegetables and fruits before adding them to soups and stocks. Place them in a bowl and add boiling water to cover. You will need to let them stand in the water for from 5 to 15 minutes to soften completely. Stir occasionally with a fork, and add more boiling water if all the water has been absorbed. Drain, reserving water to add to soup pot, and use as is or cut as directed in recipe.

You may reconstitute any number of vegetables together if they are to be added to the soup or stock at the same time. Also, measures need not be exact, but do be aware of how lightweight dehydrated fruits and vegetables are. For example, one ounce of dehydrated tomato slices numbers 16, or approximately three fresh whole tomatoes.

The dehydrator can also be used for drying garden-fresh herbs. Simply dry the sprigs, remove the leaves and crumble them and store in airtight containers. The flavor of these dried herbs will be much stronger than commercially dried ones, so use caution when adding to soups and other dishes. You may also leave the dried sprigs intact to make a bouquet garni when your herb garden has waned.

A home dehydrator is a good investment.

183

CREAM OF CABBAGE SOUP

Serves 4

1/4 ounce dehydrated leeks
1/8 ounce dehydrated green
  or red bell pepper rings
1/2 ounce dehydrated
  mushroom slices
1/2 ounce dehydrated cabbage
2 to 3 tablespoons rendered
  chicken fat and/or butter
3 to 4 cups stock or broth
Crumbled mixed dried herbs
1 cup milk or half-and-half
  cream
1 teaspoon fresh lemon juice,
  or to taste
Salt and black pepper to taste
Minced fresh parsley

Reconstitute vegetables, drain
and reserve liquid. Chop vegetables and cook, covered, in
chicken fat 10 minutes, stirring often. Add reserved liquid,
stock and herbs. Cover, bring
to boil, lower heat and cook
at gentle boil 15 minutes or
until vegetables are soft. Purée
and reheat with milk, lemon
juice and salt and pepper.
Adjust seasonings. Garnish
with parsley.

TOMATO-BROCCOLI PUREE

Serves 6

3/4 ounce dehydrated
  broccoli spears
1/2 ounce dehydrated
  mushroom slices
1/2 ounce dehydrated red
  onion slices
3 tablespoons rendered
  chicken fat and/or butter
4 to 6 cups stock or broth
1 large baking potato,
  unpeeled and diced
Crumbled dried herbs
1/2 to 3/4 ounce dehydrated
  tomato slices, reconstituted
Salt and black pepper to taste
1 to 2 cups half-and-half
  cream (optional)
Minced fresh chives

Combine broccoli, mushrooms
and onion and reconstitute.
Drain, reserving liquid, and
chop. Cook, covered, in chick-
en fat 10 minutes, stirring
often. Add reserved liquid,
stock, potato and herbs. Cover,
bring to boil, lower heat and
cook at gentle boil 15 minutes
or until vegetables are soft.
Add reconstituted tomatoes
and liquid last 5 minutes.
Season with salt and pepper,
heat with cream if using and
serve with a sprinkling of
chives.

*Dehydrate vegetables and
herbs when they are in season,
then store in airtight containers for future use.*

Glossary

The following may be found in stores that specialize in specific national cuisines and in many supermarkets and natural-foods stores.

AJI OIL Chili oil; sesame oil with cayenne pepper.

AKAMISO Red miso. See MISO.

BEAN-THREAD NOODLES Also called peastarch, shining, cellophane and transparent noodles. Opaque fine white noodle made from ground mung beans. Sold in bundles by weight.

BLACK BEANS Two varieties, Oriental and Latin American. The former are round, about 1/4 inch in diameter and black throughout, while the latter are oval with white centers.

BLACK FUNGUS Also called cloud ear, brown fungus, tree fungus and wood ear. Irregularly shaped; expands 5 to 6 times of original size and becomes gelatinous when soaked in water.

BLANCHING Parboiling 1 to 3 minutes, then draining. When used to partially cook vegetables, a cold-water rinse stops cooking at the desired point. When blanching scum-prone ingredients, such as veal bones and pig's feet, rinse well after draining, then add to fresh cooking water in a clean pot.

BOEMBOE GODOK Mixed Indonesian spices.

BOUQUET GARNI Wrap vegetables and herbs specified in cheesecloth, leaving the string long enough for easy removal.

CHINESE CHIVES Flat-leaf chive with slight garlic flavor. Easily grown.

CORIANDER, FRESH Pungent herb with leaf that resembles flat-leaf parsley. Also called cilantro and Chinese parsley. Easily grown.

FILE POWDER Powdered sassafras leaves.

FISH SOY Also called fish sauce. Pungent extract made from fish and water.

GOBO Burdock root. Long, thin brown root. Remove brown skin by rubbing with a vegetable brush or scraping with a dull knife.

HOISIN SAUCE Thick dark sauce of soybeans, chili pepper, garlic and spices. Available in cans or bottles.

JUJUBES Small dried red dates slightly sweet in flavor. Sold by weight.

JULIENNE Cutting meat or vegetables into matchstick-size pieces.

KAMABOKO Steamed loaf of fish forcemeat. Sold on wooden block wrapped in plastic in refrigerator case.

KATSUOBOSHI Dried bonito shavings. Sold by weight.

KIM CHEE Korean-style pickled cabbage.

KOMBU Dried sheet kelp.

LOP CHIANG Chinese pork sausage.

LOTUS ROOT Tuberous stem of the water lily. Sold fresh, canned or dried. Dried roots almost triple in size when soaked in water.

MATSUTAKEFU Dried, flavored wheat-flour cakes. Sold by weight.

MIRIN Sweet rice wine.

MISO Fermented paste made of malt, salt and soybeans. Available in plastic tubs or packages.

MUSHROOMS, FOREST Dried black (winter) mushrooms. Sold by weight.

NAME-TAKE Tiny mushrooms with stems. Sold in bottles.

NEEDLES Also called golden needles, lily flowers or buds, lotus petals and tiger lilies. Dried, highly nutritious flower petals. Have musky, slightly sweet flavor.

OYSTER SAUCE Thick oyster-flavored sauce. Available in cans and bottles.

PIMENTON Spanish paprika more strongly flavored than domestic variety.

RENDERING FAT To render meat or chicken fat, mince and melt over medium heat. Cool, pour into individual ice cube holders or small containers and refrigerate or freeze.

SEAWEED Dried kelp in bulk or sheet form. Doubles in size when soaked in water. Sold by weight.

SEREHPOEDER Lemon grass powder.

SHICHIMI Seven-spice mixture that includes red pepper, white sesame seeds, seaweed, mandarin orange peel, ground pod of prickly ash and black hemp seeds. Available in bottles.

SHIRATAKI NOODLES Thin yam noodles. Available fresh in tubs or canned.

SHIROMISO White miso. See MISO.

SHRIMP, DRIED Tiny dried shrimp with concentrated flavor.

SOUR SALT Citric acid.

SOYBEAN CURD Also called bean curd, bean cakes and tofu. Smooth, bland, creamy purée of soybeans formed into cakes. Also available dried in thin sheets.

TANGERINE PEEL, DRIED Dried tangerine, mandarin orange or orange peel with concentrated flavor. Sold by weight.

TOFU See SOYBEAN CURD.

TURNIP GREENS, DRIED Turnips and tops preserved with salt, dried and rolled.

Low-Calorie Substitutions

Cut the calories in your soups by making any of the following substitutions for high-calorie dairy products.

● Combine 1 cup low-fat cottage or ricotta cheese, 1 cup low-fat milk and 2 to 3 tablespoons noninstant non-fat dry milk (optional) in blender or processor. Or combine 2 cups low-fat milk or whole milk and 2/3 cup non-instant nonfat dry milk in blender or processor. Whirl until smooth. Use as substitute for half-and-half cream or evaporated milk.

● Combine 1 cup low-fat ricotta cheese, 1/4 cup plain yoghurt and 1 tablespoon noninstant low-fat milk in blender or processor. Whirl until smooth, but not foamy. Use as substitute for sour cream.

186

Index

Biographical Notes

CORALIE CASTLE is a food consultant and the author of nine other cookbooks, with more than three decades of experience in developing new recipes and innovative adaptions of classic dishes. Among her best-sellers are *Soup, The Hors d'Oeuvre Book, Real Bread,* and *The Complete Book of Steam Cookery.* An active member of the International Association of Culinary Professionals and the American Institute of Wine and Food, Ms. Castle has made numerous appearances on TV and radio to discuss food and gardening. When not traveling abroad to collect ideas and recipes for her books, she lives in Marin County, California, where she and her husband tend a one-acre garden filled with fruits, vegetables, herbs, and edible flowers.

ROY KILLEEN practiced architecture for many years before he and his wife, Jackie, started their own publishing company in 1968—101 Productions. Illustrator of a number of other books including *Bread & Breakfast, Pots & Pans Etc., Country Inns of the Far West, Country Inns of the Great Lakes* and the series of *Best Restaurant*™ guides, Roy Killeen is also the creator of the MiniMansion® series of architectural kits.